LAST NIGHT, A
SUPERHERO
SAVED MY LIFE

LAST NIGHT, A SUPERHERO SAVED MY LIFE

Neil Gaiman, Jodi Picoult, Brad Meltzer, and an All-Star Roster on the Caped Crusaders That Changed Their Lives

EDITED BY

Liesa Mignogna

THOMAS DUNNE BOOKS
ST. MARTIN'S PRESS ☙ NEW YORK

THOMAS DUNNE BOOKS.
An imprint of St. Martin's Press.

LAST NIGHT, A SUPERHERO SAVED MY LIFE. Copyright © 2016 by Liesa Mignogna. All rights reserved.
Printed in the United States of America. For information, address St. Martin's Press, 175 Fifth Avenue,
New York, N.Y. 10010.

www.thomasdunnebooks.com
www.stmartins.com

Designed by Jonathan Bennett

Library of Congress Cataloging-in-Publication Data

Names: Mignogna, Liesa editor.
Title: Last night, a superhero saved my life : Neil Gaiman, Jodi Picoult, Brad Meltzer, and an
    all-star roster on the caped crusaders that changed their lives / edited by Liesa Mignogna.
Description: First edition. | New York : Thomas Dunne Books, 2016.
Identifiers: LCCN 2015051264 | ISBN 978-1-250-04392-4 (hardback) |
    ISBN 978-1-4668-4226-7 (e-book)
Subjects: LCSH: Superheroes in literature. | Comic books, strips, etc.—History and criticism. |
    Superheroes—Psychological aspects. | BISAC: COMICS & GRAPHIC NOVELS / Nonfiction. |
    LITERARY COLLECTIONS / Essays.
Classification: LCC PN6714 .L37 2016 | DDC 741.5/352—dc23
LC record available at http://lccn.loc.gov/2015051264

Our books may be purchased in bulk for promotional, educational, or business use. Please contact
your local bookseller or the Macmillan Corporate and Premium Sales Department at 1-800-221-
7945, extension 5442, or by e-mail at MacmillanSpecialMarkets@macmillan.com.

First Edition: June 2016

10 9 8 7 6 5 4 3 2 1

COPYRIGHT ACKNOWLEDGMENTS

For Lee Franklin Mignogna,
may you never need Batman the way I did,
but always know he's there

CONTENTS

CONTENTS

X

INTRODUCTION

This is not a book about superheroes.

It's a book about the relationship between humans and superheroes—the three-dimensional, and sometimes life-sustaining dynamic between us and the iconic characters who started out on the pages of four-color comic books.

The idea for this anthology came about because of a question I'm asked all the time:

Why Batman?

I hear it from coworkers when they step into my office. First they notice the Batman notepads and pens on my desk. Then the miniature Batman figurine resting on top of my computer or the Batman mouse pad next to it. Once they turn around, that's when their eyebrows *really* shoot up—I have an entire bookshelf filled with Batman books, a Batman clock, a signed production still from the Batman animated series, and much more.

I hear it whenever someone comes over to my house and sees the guest bedroom, which doubles as the Batman room, housing my massive collection of comics, original framed art, statues, and toys. And if they stay over, they sleep underneath Batman bedding, then wake up to coffee served in a Batman mug.

I definitely heard it around the time of my wedding, when I told people that the reception would be held at a comics museum and the wedding cake would be a three-foot-long Batmobile with Just Married on the bumper and Batman and Catwoman stargazing on the front hood (no, I did not wear a cowl for the ceremony).

But what people really want to know isn't just why Batman's my favorite superhero—it's why I even *have* a favorite superhero. Why out of the entire spectrum of literature and film and culture, it's a comic book character who's become so central. I'm a reader by passion and by trade, having devoured hundreds and hundreds of books ever since preschool, eventually becoming an editor of children's and teen fiction. I've got plenty of stories to choose from, but it's Batman whose story has proven so inspiring, and so enduring.

As I shared with people why I needed a hero, and why Batman was the hero I needed, others would tell me about their own reasons for loving the Caped Crusader. And if it wasn't Batman whose mythology had made a personal impact, it was Daredevil or Spider-Man or Captain America. The connections weren't always as dramatic as my own. People shared stories of childhood escapades with capes and rooftops. They told me that geeking out over superhero comics is what bonded them to their best friends and what helped them laugh their way through their adolescence. An artist friend of mine (who contributed an essay to this book) showed me his

Superman tattoo and explained that he'd always loved the idea of a guy like Superman—someone with near-limitless abilities—using those powers to help perfectly ordinary people, even trying to fit in with those ordinary people under the guise of the ever-awkward Clark Kent. Maybe being a regular guy is cooler than we thought. . . .

The more people opened up to me, the more I realized that I was far from the only adult with a favorite super-hero, and that we all had unique and compelling reasons as to why those superheroes had come to fill that space in our lives. I'm an editor, so I'm always looking for a good story, and suddenly it was clear—

There's a story here.

Our cultural love affair with the superhero genre is no secret. Box office blockbuster lists are consistently led by superhero films like the *Avengers* and *Iron Man* franchises, not to mention the runaway success of the *Dark Knight* trilogy. During his first presidential campaign, Barack Obama revealed that he was a comic book collector and that Spider-Man was his favorite super-hero. Why Spider-Man? Because of Peter Parker's "inner turmoil."

Beneath the box office successes, the fanboy politicians, even the popular "spot the Superman reference in every episode of *Seinfeld*" game, are the human connections we form with these characters and the question:

Why superheroes?

As I reached out to authors and they leaped (tall

buildings) at the chance to write about their favorite superheroes, a few themes emerged.

For some writers, there was a common ground that tied back to the notion of values, morality, a *code*. Understanding the characters' strengths and their flaws in comparison to and contrasted with our own as humans was deeply inspiring. The form that inspiration took was sometimes daunting, sometimes heartening, sometimes comforting—but always helping to offer a context in which the authors could better understand both super and human limitations, and learn how to accept and embrace them.

Two authors shared stories about how they were influenced by superhero couples, and another talked about finding his first love in a comic book. In the romantic entanglements of the all-powerful, these authors found insight about their own taste, a bittersweet sense of familiarity, and even a tenuous reason to believe that love could actually save the day. Another author found love not for a person but for a city that would one day become his home.

It was also interesting that a few contributors could point specifically to superheroes as the reason they even became writers in the first place.

With all the focus on their larger-than-life abilities and (typically) perfect bodies, it makes sense that several writers focused on how superheroes relate to questions of gender identity. I was hoping to include as diverse a cast of superheroes as possible in the collection, but there were two whose names kept coming up. One of these was Wonder Woman. Three of the eight female contributors wrote about the Amazon princess, which is really its own kind of statement. She's one of the (sadly) few prominent woman superheroes, and many women today can trace their evolving sense of sexual identity back to Wonder Woman's strength but also to her bizarrely revealing outfit, as one author here does with unflinching honesty.

So who was the second repeat superhero? I swear I didn't rig it, but, yes, of course, it was Batman—as an inspiration, as a mirror, as a lifeline. Years ago, he appeared when I needed a hero—when I'd suffered through a series of traumatic experiences and felt completely alone and scared. His story saved my story.

So why superheroes?

Because maybe they really do show up whenever you need them.

Even in real life.

SUPERHEROES
AND BEING HUMAN

ME AND BATMAN AND YOU

AUSTIN GROSSMAN

> This is a song about how sometimes you find yourself living in a house where you think "I have to get out of here" but maybe you're too young to get out of there, or you don't have any money, or you don't have any means or anywhere to go, and yet you cling firmly to the idea that someday you will escape, through some means, maybe Batman will show up in his car outside or something. And like other people might laugh and say, "Man, John, Batman's not coming to save you." And you think, "Look man, between me and Batman and you, I'll take Batman."
>
> —*John Darnielle*

I.

'll take Batman. Golden Age Batman or campy Silver Age or grim Batman or the aging Dark Knight or even Batman 2099. I'll take whoever chooses to answer the Bat-Signal on a given rainy night.

I'll take him for all sorts of reasons. Because he's a weird superhero. No powers, just his self-discipline and talent and personal hang-ups. Part vicious vigilante, part neurotic warrior saint. With his private cult of unrelenting mourning, he's the costumed patron of the walking wounded, of simply Not Getting Over It.

I'll take Batman because in the morning he makes such a point of getting up again as Bruce Wayne. He eases a tailored suit on over the bruises and eats his breakfast in bed and sallies forth into the world. He laughs lightly while cracked ribs twinge; makes witty, provocative conversation while counting the hours until sunset, feeling the anguish of knowing how many crimes are even then taking place. Friends wonder why he's always a little remote, why he always happens to know the phase of the moon and the likelihood of rain on a given night in Gotham. The scourge of crime plays it arrow straight; he freezes at the slightest danger of discovery, like a kid caught without a hall pass. Because he takes all of it a little too seriously, including—especially—the most absurd parts of it.

I've got questions for the man. Because really, Bruce, what's going on? Is everything okay? Why the night job, why the lifelong free-running fistfight in a Halloween suit? And, I know, I know, it's for your parents, it's for two dead people who really truly aren't coming back. It's just Batman's luck to be born into the doomful DC Universe where permadeath is the norm instead of Marvel's revolving-door afterlife, where Tom and Martha Wayne (or their good-as-new clones) would have shown up again on Tuesday next in time for cocktail hour. Sorry, Bruce. In DC's world, only Clark Kent comes back.

And while we're asking questions, we could always ask why, at my time of life, do I bank so hard on the possibility of intervention by a costumed vigilante rather than, say, a skilled accountant or psychiatrist?

And, most pressing of all, damn it: Is Batman coming to save me, or isn't he? Who's going to solve the disastrous supercrime scenario of my middle years, if not the World's Greatest Detective?

II.

If I'm calling Batman a neurotic, I don't mean to cast aspersions. Of course Batman is a mess. I'm a mess, too. Lots of us are messes. That's why we like Batman, the hero with something broken.

The thing is, not all of us have Bruce Wayne's excuse for falling off the path to middle-class normalcy. With him, it makes sense to have issues. Billionaire kid, parents gunned down on a moonlit night, who wouldn't have a few quirks? You can at least point to the problem. For the rest of us it takes a little more work.

Like plenty of Batman fans, I don't have quite such an obvious piece of melodrama to explain things. We had a nice house in a quiet safe suburb. Middle-class school, good marks, pleasant surroundings. College education, even. Parents totally not shot. So whatever went wrong in my life, well, that's a harder case to crack. The crime scene is immaculate. Witnesses never saw a thing.

Likewise, Batman's break with the regular college-bound achievement track was pretty easy to spot. In his teens, he ran away from his palatial suburban mansion on a quest to remake himself. He mastered physics, chemistry, engineering, forensic sciences. He roamed Asia and studied a dozen different martial disciplines.

If only we all had that great story, a Crime Alley that led us to our brooding midnight dysfunction. Instead, some of us get a wandering path. It looked like all systems were go, but then down the line there was a more subtle, creeping failure to launch. Wandering from job to job, relationship to relationship via a series of crappy little apartments, never decorated, boxes never unpacked. It's easy not to ask questions when you still think you're smart and successful, but you can go into your thirties to find no actual career or marriage has formed, and gradually suspect the wheels are coming right off the cart.

So what happened? Some say the perfect crime is the one that no one ever knows happened. No one sees anything wrong, not for years. All of a sudden you're in your late thirties and the bodies really start piling up and you look around to find the city of Gotham has become a very dark and terrifying place. Parents dead or alive, there are evidently lots of smaller, more ordinary ways for someone's life to end up broken.

By whose dire hand was this done? Surely no ordinary malefactor was at work here. Was this perhaps the work of the Riddler? Certainly the landscape was littered with lasting riddles. Why are things that are simple and obvious to other people—remaining in a job, for instance, or paying one's taxes correctly—mysterious or just about impossible to me? Why am I doing the same stupid thing over and over? Why are my friends asking whether I'm okay, and do I know how I sound, and do I know what I look like right now? I should probably know those answers, but then I am not exactly the World's Greatest Detective. (*Or am I? Stay tuned for the shocking truth.*)

It's very late in the day to be calling Commissioner Gordon for a rooftop meeting, and not in the finest weather either. But look, there's the Bat-Signal all plugged in and sitting there. So . . . what if I maybe just shine that thing up at the clouds, like a movie premiere or a sale on automobiles. Just for a sec, no commitment, just in an exploratory way. To see how things go, and who shows up. What have I got to lose?

III.

My Batman obsession began in earnest when I read *The Dark Knight Returns* in 1986, the year it came out. It was a galvanizing moment, a purging aesthetic revelation that expanded my sense of what was possible in the world of art, as powerful as the moment I heard punk rock or put a quarter in a Defender machine or saw a Bob Fosse dance routine. I didn't have the slightest idea why I felt that way, but I did. I kept my copy through college and grad school and various forgotten intervals between, read it a couple of times a year at least.

The book finds Bruce Wayne in later life; he's been retired for ten years but the Batman thing won't leave him alone. He can't shed the memories of what happened and what he needs to do about it. He's fighting it out nightly with himself, sweating into the sheets. *I'm a zombie,* he says, *a Flying Dutchman. A dead man, ten years dead.* Battling crime was what made sense of him, and his life has no meaning without it.

It was a sentiment I understood too well, even without knowing why. It told me a story about myself that fit my feelings while having no relationship to the facts. I read *The Dark Knight Returns* over and over until I had extensive patches of it memorized, long after Frank Miller had turned himself into a caricatured irrelevancy. I read it in college and in my twenties and in my thirties as I shed jobs and apartments, as early promise turned into a wistful memory, then an angry regret. The conundrum of my failure to thrive in the world went from quirky to worrisome to saddening, and the rootless-slacker thing got less and less cute.

Why does Batman make so much sense to me? This is my question, and this is the basis of my hope. Because maybe he will, after all, show up to save me.

Bruce Wayne is a mess but give him this: he pulled it together. He grew up and now manages something like a borderline okay adulthood. He's managed to convince everyone he's okay, and that's no mean trick when you are not, in fact, even remotely okay.

His parents got murdered when he was just a kid and humiliatingly powerless to stop it, and that memory just does not go away, not ever.

He had a problem, and he came up with a plan. Not

that he had to—he was rich enough to keep himself in therapy for a dozen lifetimes, with yachts and movie stars to fill in the intervening hours and stave off the awfulness. But, no, he took what happened to him, packaged it up, and turned it into a lifestyle.

Let's not pretend it was the cleverest thing he could have come up with: it was a very silly plan. When he came back from his years abroad, he decided to become a superhero. He put a mask on his face, I guess inspired by the movie *The Mark of Zorro*. But if adulthood teaches us one good sharp lesson, it's that even if an unconventional piece of clothing looks great on someone in a movie that doesn't mean you run out and buy a whole new outfit. I've owned enough fedoras to have learned that particular truth.

He wears the mask. He sits on rooftops at all hours, rides around town in a weird car. He beats the crap out of bad people basically because he's sad and angry. And at that point he'll really cut loose. He'll grab a guy's hair and shove his face into a brick wall; he'll kick a guy's knee out. If Batman catches you doing the wrong thing, you can forget about playground rules. Don't even try calling a time-out.

Take note, he's not even pretending this is going to fix it. This is the thing that makes him feel closest to whole, but that's all it's going to be, ever. This is the deal for him and he'll be doing it the rest of his life. "Get used to it," says Batman. "It's not just a phase."

And you know what? The plan works. Like the best friend who has suddenly gotten way too into remote-control helicopters, who turns out to have sunk five thousand dollars into scale-model Hueys and doesn't remotely regret it. It's getting him by, and who are we to judge?

IV.

Meanwhile the investigation grinds on, stray crumbs of evidence that stubbornly refuse to form the wholesome bread of justice!

Where were we? I moved from Boston to New York, to Boston, to Los Angeles, to Brooklyn, to San Francisco, to Southern California. I cut myself off from my family, my friends. I felt as if I were hiding a terrible secret but I didn't know what the secret was, only that it had just about finished gnawing my insides out.

In fact I bore a more than passing resemblance to our playboy millionaire. He's no stranger to secrets hidden in plain sight. You could know Bruce Wayne your whole life and never suspect that he had another side to him. If you were going to spot him, the real clue is in the eyes, alert and haunted, scanning the room, knowing that this charming party we're all enjoying could flip over into a hellscape of smilex gas and panicked society matrons; in fact in Gotham the odds are sixty-forty on a given evening. Bruce Wayne is suspiciously at home with the possibility of disaster.

Like Bruce Wayne I smiled an empty-eyed smile and

raised a festive glass as the confetti rained down and the

band played a jazzy tune. And all the while, far below the glamorous heights of Gotham's financial district, a chill autumn breeze carried eerie laughter through the deserted streets. An alarm bell rang and rang past emptied display cases. Something had been taken and it wasn't being given back. The weed of crime bears bitter fruit! And someone awfully sick was finding this awfully funny.

In fact it got harder and harder to care, or take any of it seriously. Every relationship that happened because I didn't imagine a better offer coming, and besides, they wanted it so much, right? Every freelance job where I didn't ask for a proper rate, because what did it matter? The ones where I didn't bother to collect payment. And every time I quit writing because, really, what are the odds that I turn out to be one of the lucky ones?

There was nothing, no work or friendship I could turn my hand to that didn't sooner or later start to feel like a sour joke. Who could be behind my unfortunate demise? Who but the Clown Prince of Crime himself?

V.

And who else could save me but Batman? As a former Ph.D. student in English literature, I know as well as you do what a silly suggestion that is. Why not read a story with real people and real human feelings, or whatever is in all those Henry James novels that's meant to be so important?

I've read my Henry James and George Eliot, those masterful literary instructors in the slow task of maturation, adjustment of expectations, accommodation to realities.

But that's exactly the kind of lesson I was already way too good at. Yielding to disappointment was a topic I had intimate familiarity with. And Henry James wasn't coming to save me anytime soon—it's just not his style. So who would? Batman, that's who.

In my twenties I began a master's degree in performance studies at NYU, an honor with an almost perfect lack of applicability to any of my real-world problems. I was living on almost nothing. I was reading almost nothing except critical theory and Batman. I didn't know what I was doing there.

I started a small, secret ritual. Each night around ten in the evening I'd head over to the School for the Arts, flash my ID to get in, and wait as gradually the black box rehearsal spaces emptied out and the undergrad theater majors went back to their dorms. I'd try until I found one unlocked and unoccupied. I'd switch on the stage lights and sit up there and write in a spiral notebook, then read the result aloud to the ranks of empty seats.

I don't know why I did it that way, but I had to hear my voice echoing off the walls of a room, and until then it didn't feel real. Until then, it felt like nothing. But reading it out at the center of an empty room . . . then it felt halfway like a crime, halfway like a miserable, joyous duty to a demon inside me I couldn't explain. It felt ridiculous and it felt like anger.

No one was trying to kill me at that point and if I tried I could probably have kept from starving to death, so don't ask me why the whole enterprise was running itself into the ground. Also the writing sucked, it would go on sucking for the next ten years, it's a published novel now and right this minute it may be out there sucking. It was, moreover, ridiculous—as anyone who has seen my prose fiction can confirm. Nevertheless it felt very much like a struggle to save my own life, and so far it has. I went out at night and did the only thing that made sense, the scariest, most ridiculous, most courageous thing I could summon myself to do. So was this the work of the elusive Batman, rumored scourge of the underworld? This humble reporter has no other explanation to give. Bruce Wayne's story was the closest thing I could find to a story about caring what happened to me.

I wrote the first pages of my first novel when I was twenty-six. It took until my thirties that I picked it up and wrote it, over a long six years, in between classes and Saturday nights in donut shops, hidden away from my younger classmates in a doctoral program I wasn't going to finish. I was published at thirty-seven and the book did modestly well.

Okay. So I'm not much like Batman. Then again, neither is Bruce Wayne. And you've never seen me and Batman in the same place either.

So is Batman coming or not? What would that even look like? I'm not sure we get an answer here, or even a happy ending. After all, Bruce Wayne doesn't get one and Batman certainly doesn't. The World's Greatest Detective will never get over letting his parents down, no more than I will. And in the years that followed, parts of my behavior got worse, not better.

But at least I know something about fighting crime. I know the opposite of depression isn't happiness, it's vitality and truth and the snap of bone in a thug's elbow as you pull a joint lock home. My second book did not sell as well as the first. My third may be the best so far. At least I know a story about how someone failed the people he loved, felt hollow and useless, and then did something about it.

This essay should logically end in my own secret, the place where my own thoughts and energy and life go when I'm not walking around pretending to be who I am, my own personal Crime Alley. What's the story there? Dead parents? Lost ambitions? Is it simply the poisoned atmosphere on this blighted alien planet I've been stranded on? I don't know. I don't have a good excuse for not being a normal person with decent, respectable imperatives. You'll have to wait for *Secret Origins of Fortysomething Writers 2.*

If you're going to be a Batman fan, you're in touch with the irrational, with the unsolved case that never gets closed. We know that things don't change for Bruce

Wayne. He doesn't get married, unless you count Alfred. He keeps his friends at a distance, and they shrug and they know he's doing what he can with what his own history's made of him. Grimly and privately he loves the little existence he's made for himself. When he's leaping through moonlit alleyways, he feels like himself, like he is drinking from some deep personal well, night cool and intoxicating.

Maybe that's my fate—the ongoing investigation of a crime I never saw committed, whose consequences only came to light over the long years after, and maybe solving it isn't the point. When the Bat-Signal's up, you'll be out there working, probably in the rain, fighting crime until dawn.

ME AND BATMAN AND YOU

ON THE HULK

YOU WOULDN'T LIKE ME WHEN I'M ANGRY

DELILAH S. DAWSON

When I was little, I wanted to be three things: a cowboy, an artist, and the Incredible Hulk. There's even a Polaroid of me hugging a Hulk punching bag I got for Christmas, love and worship shining in my smile. The funny thing is that all three wishes actually came true. I love my horse, I'm a writer, and I have more in common with Bruce Banner's dangerous side than I'd like to admit. What I wanted so much as a child were power and invincibility, but what I actually found was a hidden core of indestructible rage that made me a better artist, person, and mother.

Everybody knows about the Incredible Hulk: a smart young doctor gets blasted with gamma radiation. After that, whenever he gets too angry, he turns into a giant green rage monster who's mostly invulnerable and breaks everything in his path. According to the latest version of *The Avengers*, the good doctor at one point admits that he grew so despondent about his inner Hulk that he put a gun in his mouth and pulled the trigger, and the Hulk spit out the bullet. I tried something similar when I was a teen, but here I am today, patiently explaining to two small clones of myself the differences between the X-Men and the Avengers, Marvel and DC.

I still recall the anger I felt as a child. Although I know I watched a lot of the *Hulk* TV show with my parents, the two main images I retain are of the Hulk getting angry and breaking things . . . and the broken man walking along a deserted highway, mournful and alone. Even when I was very little, I could relate to both moments. Loneliness and rage go hand in hand.

As young as four, I can remember railing against injustice, beating my fists against my locked bedroom door when I didn't get my way. My mom tells the story that while I was inside, screaming my rage at her, she was outside, throwing rocks at the side of the house until she pulled her shoulder. But we were no match for my father. On the outside, he was a six-foot-two bodybuilder with glasses as thick as Coke bottle bottoms, mild and friendly. But when he drank, much like Bruce Banner's father, his own beast came forward. There were nights I spent with a chair pushed under my doorknob. There were nights I was choked almost unconscious and told that I should've been born a boy. And, once I was old enough, there were nights that I stared past him to the garage door, running mental calculations regarding how drunk he was and whether I could get my keys and jump into the car fast enough to peel out of the driveway before he finally followed up on his threat to kill me.

When I was seventeen, I went to France with a school exchange program. I'd never been on an airplane, much less out of the country, and my parents were opposed to the experience. I saved up, working part time, and paid for it myself. Once I landed on the other side of the Atlantic, I felt like a different person. No one in France knew who I was or cared that I hadn't been born a male athlete. My host family welcomed me into their home and treated me like their fourth daughter. There were three meals a day, no snacking, and no fridge full of beer. When they argued, it was in the spirit of intelligent debate, and I marveled at how *Maman* and Papa listened to their children and treated them like equals. When my father argued with me, he made me sit on a low stool on the floor as he towered above me. I was not allowed to talk back.

My host family treated me to several holidays, and we were staying on the beach in Biarritz when I realized that I would soon have to go back home. That my opinion would no longer be valued and that each night at my house could suddenly and without warning become a drunken list of my faults, a screaming match, or red lights flashing behind my eyes while the choke hold came on. I would go back to being a prisoner of the Hulk. Two Hulks, actually: my father's alcoholism and my own rage, which I had always kept hidden.

Out on the beach, my host student said she was going to go take a nap under the umbrella and asked if I wanted to join her. I looked back at her family: Papa, snoring. *Maman,* reading a romance book. The little sisters, building a sand castle. They were so peaceful, so comfortable with one another. So easy. My family had never been that way. So I told her I wanted to go back into the ocean.

I waded into the warm water and started swimming. And when the shelf dropped out and the water grew colder, I didn't stop. I kept on. I wanted to swim forever. I wanted to be Edna Pontellier from *The Awakening,* gently giving up and having it be her choice because it was the last choice she got to make. If going home was the only thing I could do, then I wasn't going to do it. My lungs began to burn, and the waves got choppier, and my arms ached, and I kept going. The horizon was forever away, the sun a white dot. The laughter and splashing on the shore was long gone, and the water below me was no longer clear and blue. It was black and dark and cold, fathomless. But I didn't stop.

I am a strong swimmer. I love the water. I feel at home there. And I thought that drowning would be like going to sleep, like pulling a cozy blanket over your head and sinking into bliss.

I stopped swimming.

I closed my eyes.

I exhaled.

I sank.

I wanted to die, so badly.

I wanted all the pain to be over with. The worry. The fear. The never knowing how each day would end and constant painful awareness that it wasn't in my power to decide. The always being good, following all the rules, tiptoeing through life, and still getting beat down.

I remember how cold and peaceful and dark it was underwater. Down under the waves, there's just a gentle rocking as you float. As you sink.

But the thing is, when you have a Hulk inside you, sometimes the monster's not ready to give up. Sometimes the monster spits out the bullet. Or, in my case, the Hulk kicks to the surface, flails your limbs toward the shore, and gets thrown onto the sand, coughing up gallons of water.

I tell you now that I did not have the energy to swim back. I swam as hard as I could to get out that far, as far as I could. I'd done it on purpose—so that I *couldn't* swim back. My muscles were jelly. I didn't want to live. I swear that as I lay half in, half out of the waves, unwillingly alive, I pounded my fist against the sand and cried until the sobs turned into laughter.

Something happens to a person when they beat death. When you've looked into the abyss and the abyss has looked back and you're on speaking terms, you know that you can face anything and come out the other side. That doesn't mean it's easy. That doesn't mean the world can't hurt you, that it won't hurt you. It just means you know you can win.

As soon as I could move, I splashed the tears away and dragged myself to the family umbrella. Papa was still snoring, *Maman* was still reading, little sisters had a magnificent palace studded with shells, and my host student was, as promised, napping. No one had even noticed that I was gone, much less that I had done my damnedest to kill myself on their watch.

I flopped on my back in the sand, feeling as fresh and new as a blank sheet of paper, as if I'd left some part of myself out there in the ocean like a spent cocoon. It felt like playing a video game, when your guy dies, and you respawn in the same place with a new guy.

The first thing I noticed was how hot the sun felt on my hair. And then I noticed the breeze on my skin. When was the last time I'd noticed such feelings? One by one, I started to catalog reasons that I was glad to be alive, things I would've missed if I'd succeeded and sunk. On the way home from the beach, I asked to stop at a stationery store, where I bought a notebook and a pen and began writing down all the things that I loved, from summer grass under bare feet to cold bedsheets in winter to bright blue, cloudless skies. That night's simple seaside dinner of fried haddock and white rice remains one of the most delicious things I've ever eaten.

Years later, when I watched *Fight Club* and Tyler Durden said, "Tomorrow will be the most beautiful day of Raymond K. Hessel's life," I understood completely.

When I went back home at the end of the summer, nothing had changed. But I had. It was easier, somehow, to deal with the everyday anxiety, to put on a bland mask and take whatever was dished out. Deep down, I was untouchable. What was the worst thing that could happen? I'd already tasted Death's bullet and spit it back out. Some monstrous, unbeatable, utterly indestructible beast inside me was willing to rise and bypass my brain and heart to keep going, even when the rest of me had given up. Instead of rejecting my Hulk, I embraced it.

One night, my dad got drunker than usual. He took it too far. He hit my mom for the first time. And my Hulk stood me up from that stool, marched me to my keys, and put me behind the wheel of my car, where I kept a bugout bag for exactly this eventuality. I didn't run, like I'd always imagined. I walked. Step by step, not turning around, knowing that there was something even more honest and damning in my deadly calm as I left that house, I walked. Because I was done being scared.

It wasn't a good year. A few months later, an ex-boyfriend stalked me, cornered me, and raped me in my best friend's basement. He had a knife; he was unstable; and there was no one there to hear me scream, even before he put a hand over my mouth. But as we struggled, as he wedged a knee between my thighs, I stilled. Deep down inside, that same deadly calm settled. He couldn't touch me. He couldn't stop me. He couldn't take anything from me. I wouldn't let him. I retreated into my mind, floated to the ceiling, and watched his back pumping in his white undershirt. And it hurt in a thousand different ways, but I lived through it.

For a long time, I felt guilty, like I should've fought back harder. If I was so strong, if my Hulk was so powerful, why had I not fought my attacker with fists and elbows and teeth? The Hulk, as we know him, is a savage, mindless beast who sometimes can't discriminate between friend and foe. But the Hulk I carry inside me is more cunning and thoughtful—if just as indestructible. I don't know what would've happened to me if I had fought my attacker, but I do know the life I gained by staying alive through the assault. It took many years for me to accept that surviving is the best revenge.

The last time I encountered my Hulk was while giving birth to my second child. My daughter had been a surprise C-section for breech, but I was able to have a natural birth for my son. I am not, as they say, a good birther. I screamed and cried and yelled at people in French; and at one point, I came to the tipping point between animal and human, a place without words and only pain and darkness that I think must connect every mother going back to our days in the caves. I met my Hulk there, and we looked eye to eye, and I knew that I could get through anything. That I was unbreakable. That the only way out is through. And with one more push, my son entered the world.

The funny thing is this: my son inherited my Hulk. He's six now, a child of great joy and exuberance who can't hold still and dances through life. But when he gets angry, he can't control his emotions. He bends over, his hands in shaking fists, his teeth bared, growling. My

husband's anger can't pull him out of it. My mother's
calm reasoning can't break the spell.

I am the only one who can calm his Hulk.

It has to happen sideways: a tickle game, a hug, wearing a funny hat. You can't fight the Hulk; you have to charm the Hulk, lure the Hulk, love the Hulk no matter how angry he is and no matter what he says. When you're the smallest person in the family, it can be easy to feel powerless. And pretending he's the Hulk is how my son claims his anger, claims his space. Being the Hulk allows him to be heard.

And so I let him own his feelings, air his grievances, and even use words that hurt to express himself. I don't put him on a stool and make him look up at me, listen to me tell him how to act. I don't tell him what's wrong with his feelings, what's wrong with who he is as a person. I don't want his anger to become this flaming, unbreakable core of bottled-up rage from years of not being heard and feeling powerless.

I just hug him.

"I love you, Hulk," I say.

"I love you, too, Mama Hulk," he says back.

Because what I want him to know is this: it's okay to be angry. Hell, it's even okay to be angry *all the time*, as Mark Ruffalo's Bruce Banner admits to Tony Stark, because there's a lot in the world that's worthy of rage. It's okay to have feelings and express them. It's okay to be who you are and do what you want to do, as long as you're not hurting anyone. It's okay to mess up, because messing up is the first step to being great. Bruce Banner is scared to form bonds with other people because at any time, the Hulk might erupt and hurt the people he loves. I want my son to know that I will love his sweet side and his angry side, no matter what.

But words matter. And actions matter. And memories become part of you forever. People fear the Hulk, and when you fear something, you can't love it. I think that's what happened to me as a kid. As soon as my dad stopped drinking, he became a great dad, but he didn't stop drinking until I was eighteen and walked out the door.

Our relationship is wonderful now, and we don't talk about the past. I can't forget what happened, but I can forgive. And I can try to understand and do better myself. When my kids look at me, I don't want them to see the Hulk waiting to break out of a cage with one false step or wrong word, as if they are the cause and catalyst for my anger. I want them to see Dr. Banner, trying to do good in spite of his Hulk and trying, again and again, to come to terms with his dark side, to tame it, and put it to work. Which might explain a lot about the horror and high body counts in my books.

One day, when my kids are older, I'll tell them about that day in France. I'll tell them with full honesty what it felt like to drown, and what it felt like to *want* to drown. And then I'll tell them how much better it feels to live. I'll pull out that red-and-white-checkered book from France and let them read all the things that I love about being alive. And then I'll pull out the blue-and-white-checkered sequel that I started when the depression got really bad again.

Both books are full, but there's still so much more to add, if I need to.

I feel like our current society wants us to be okay, to be normal, to pretend like everything is fine. All the while, we're stuffing ourselves full of pills and beers and bigger televisions, trying to fill a chasm that never goes away. Trying to throw chemicals and money at that Hulk, hoping he won't come to the fore. Hoping that he will continue to play nicely. But the truth is that no one is normal. No one feels happy all the time. So many of us have a Hulk inside, fueled by the past and the present and worries about the future. So many of us have had a finger on the trigger, wondering if pulling it might be easier than going on. Not all of us have a monster strong enough to spit the bullet back out.

These days, I am grateful for my Hulk, mostly because I've learned to love it. That's all the Hulk wants, really. To be seen, understood, and loved. To matter. I started out loving my Hulk punching bag, but as a kid, I didn't understand that it was weighted by design. That meant that no matter how much abuse it took, it always finished the fight standing. Unbeatable.

You might not like me when I'm angry, but I like myself just fine.

DENTED HEARTS

A STORY OF IRON MAN

ANTHONY BREZNICAN

It's not strength that makes the hero. It's weakness. It's the crack in the armor.

We know this for certain deep down, even if we don't like to admit it, even if we prefer to focus on the phenomenal powers and invincibility of the comic book characters we love. Maybe we don't like to admit that our own pain or vulnerability has value. Better to shove it off into the corner, ignore its call, and pretend it doesn't exist. But sometimes the bad in our lives is what makes us yearn to be good, to fight harder.

So when I hear the name Iron Man, I don't think of the indestructible suit that encases Tony Stark's body. To me, the "iron" in that name calls to mind the inoperable fragments of metal embedded in his chest, edging forward like razor-sharp debris in a glacier, perilously close to puncturing the muscle that pumps blood through his body.

Iron Man has a bad heart. And this—not the armor—is his true strength.

It took me a long time to realize this, but a big brother and a little sister I know figured it out a lot earlier. My wife, Jill, was born with a bad heart, and her brother, Grant Piontek, protected her and cared for her long before I entered the picture. Even though he was a few years older than her—an age when most big brothers only tend to pass torment on to smaller siblings—he was the type of guy who didn't mind sharing his comic book collection full of damaged heroes, bulletproof bravery, and life-changing miracles at a time when she desperately needed strength.

Tony Stark was their hero, but the two of them—they're my heroes. So this is their story—Grant and Jill, the big strong kid and an ailing little girl. It's about the kind of friendship and love formed over a lifetime that truly is indestructible. I'd say it's a bond forged in iron, but it's actually a lot stronger than that.

Okay, so this theory of mine: Tony Stark has the high-tech, mechanical suit of armor, he can soar through the air like a fighter jet, and he's got the repulsor beams in his palms to blast away foes like you'd wave away mosquitoes. All that is devastatingly powerful, sure. But villains have power, too. Strength doesn't define good or bad. Stark built the metal suit, but that weak, vulnerable heart? That's what built the hero. Everything else is simply a . . . utility.

That calls to mind a different hero from another universe: to me, Iron Man is to Marvel what Batman is to DC. They're both what the Hulk would call "puny humans" (albeit billionaire, playboy philanthropists) with no otherworldly abilities beyond obsessive willpower and a deep-rooted scorn for injustice. It's not Bruce Wayne's money, genius, or physical prowess that make him a warrior for the right, it's the loss of his parents. It's the pain that doesn't leave him, one he hopes to spare others. It's the symbolic hole in his heart.

In Stark's case, that hole is dangerously close to being literal.

Iron Man might never have been born if an explosion hadn't pierced the sternum of weapons designer Tony Stark in 1963's *Tales of Suspense* 39. After triggering a land mine in Vietnam, he was kidnapped by the Communist warlord Wong-Chu and enslaved as a munitions maker. Let's say Stark had been captured uninjured—the shrewd engineer could've still assembled some diabolical gadget to blast himself free, but without the shrapnel in his chest, he wouldn't have had to *continue* wearing that armor. The magnetized transistors (in the movies, it's the glowing ARC reactor) were needed to draw those metallic shards away from his ticker.

Becoming a victim of a blast, being on the business end of an explosion, opened Stark's eyes to the pain his weaponry was causing others. It triggered empathy in a man who previously had none, who probably never even thought about the consequences of the devices he created. This is the value of pain. In our nervous system, it makes us withdraw from things that cut or burn or freeze or destroy. In our hearts (the metaphorical ones), pain can make us run toward those things, if only to help stop them from hurting others.

The suit kept Tony Stark alive, and that led him to dedicate his life to keeping others alive. Most of us don't ever get to do anything so dramatic, unless we're soldiers, firefighters, cops, or happen to be bystanders at some terrible accident that gives us the chance to put our own well-being aside for the sake of someone else. But in an age of selfishness and cynicism, when empathy and generosity seem to be in short supply, it's enough in the real world just to be a good guy, someone who doesn't battle supervillains but who simply goes out of his or her way to make the world a slightly more decent place. Superheroes take the good and bad we can do and just magnify it to larger-than-life perspectives. Still, we find inspiration in them, just like we have since storytelling began.

Iron Man is my favorite hero because Tony Stark could easily have gone the villain route, could easily have become Marvel's Lex Luthor instead of its Batman, but instead he became a hero thanks to that life-threatening metal embedded inside him, perpetually reminding him of his frailty, of his weakness. I have a soft spot for bad hearts, which is why Tony Stark reminds me so much of Jill and my brother-in-law, Grant. My wife's bad heart made her brother choose to be her hero.

Jill was born with tetralogy of Fallot, commonly known as a hole in the heart, which made her valves operate a little like a cracked straw. Children who are born with this defect tend to be called "blue babies" because their hearts can't deliver enough oxygen. Until my wife's generation—kids born in the late seventies—there wasn't a lot that doctors could do to help. Just like Iron Man, that terrifying threat to the heart was just something to live with. Or not live at all.

The story of Jill and Grant is the story of the eternal war between big brothers and little sisters turned upside down. As a former mean big brother myself, we definitely do *not* share our comic books with bratty little sisters. It's practically treasonous to invite younger siblings into the world of superheroes, monsters, and the cosmic secrets of the universe. But that's exactly what Grant did back around 1982, when he would've been about eleven and Jill would've been around five. He had started getting into comic books. Deep into them. Religious cult kind of deep. Over the years, he amassed a collection of thousands, and this was no passing childhood fad. When he grew up, he started putting out a Christmas tree each year decorated in nothing but superhero ornaments, and in recent years, amid this modern renaissance of comic book movies, Grant turned out for the first night of every single one of them. He was also a skydiver, car enthusiast, Harley rider, and hiker. He was a lifelong geek and adventurer who turned Jill into both of those things, too.

Grant was the middle child, and his older sister, Kelli, was also born with congenital heart problems. She underwent surgery when she was five years old to correct it, and although she made it through okay, that fear never left the household. Heart surgery on a small child is always scary, but back in those days the technology was far less advanced, and the success nowhere near certain. The Piontek family knew this devastating truth already, better than any family should.

When Jill's father was a teenager, his baby sister was also was born with a hole in her heart. A blue baby. Her name was Audrey, and she died on June 1, 1960, just two years and one month old. Almost. Her brief life ended just short of that month marker by two days.

The memory of that lost little girl consumed this family and haunts them to this day, more than five decades later. As a result, when Kelli was born, they knew how rapidly a bad situation could turn unspeakably tragic.

Kelli had her surgery, and she survived. But when Grant was born, he was the family's first fully healthy child in decades. I imagine he seemed like a miracle baby, a little Hercules, just for being normal, and he grew up knowing his health and strength were an un- usual blessing in a family cursed with faulty genes. He understood that sometimes others, like his sister Kelli, came first, because they weren't as fortunate.

When Jill was born, eight years younger than her sister and six years younger than her brother, she was even more frail and vulnerable. You can tell from the old photos of her at that age—something was wrong. She had the same bright eyes and big smile of any toddler, but she's distressingly thin and there's something in her expression that seems distant and out of place. It's fear.

Every time I look at that stretched and faded scar that still runs down the center of her chest, I think of the tiny child who overheard whispered talk of another little girl with a bad heart, a long-ago child named Audrey, who never got to grow up.

I think of Jill being wheeled into a hospital. Her parents and doctors telling her everything would be okay. But she knew that was a lie meant to reassure her. She was just a kid, but she'd heard them talking about Audrey, and she knew other little boys and girls from her floor who went in for surgery and never came back.

Jill was one of the lucky kids. She made it.

It was scary, but that little girl was tougher than she looked, and she was in the hands of some expert doctors who knew just how to stitch up a miniature heart. After the surgery, in the years that followed, the main person who helped her feel strong was her big brother. If Jill needed a heart today, she could have mine. But back then, I know Grant would have given her his.

There wasn't much Grant could do to heal his little sister medically, but he filled her life with comics that inspired her spirit—stories of people who went through horrible accidents and somehow came out stronger. Peter Parker, bitten by a spider full of radioactive toxins and spurred to a life of crime fighting by the murder of his beloved uncle. Superman, who comes to Earth with the power to do nearly anything—except save his annihilated home world of Krypton. Captain America, who also loses everything after being trapped in ice as the world he knew receded into history. Later, Jill became a librarian and loved that her profession was shared by Barbara Gordon, aka Batgirl, who was left a paraplegic by a gunshot from the Joker in 1988's *Batman: The Killing Joke* but resurrected herself to fight back in a different way as the superhacker Oracle. Comics are full of wounded people whose pain makes them stronger.

Then, of course, there was Tony Stark. The man in the metal mask. The guy whose weak spot and strong spot was right in the center of his chest.

Although I associate Grant with Iron Man, his other favorite hero was a different Marvel character: Wolverine, the cigar-chomping, tough-talking, clawed badass with the adamantium skeleton and the power to regenerate instantly. A part of me wonders if the superpowered healing had some subconscious influence over why he loved that surly member of the X-Men so much. Growing up with two sisters who fought like hell to recover from traumatic surgeries, I imagine there was something cathartic about a guy who never even needed a Band-Aid.

Everything Grant did, Jill imitated. Grant loved comics, so she loved comics. Grant played Pop Warner football, and Jill and Kelli signed on as cheerleaders. Grant took up photography in college, and so did teenage Jill.

He started studying history, and that inspired her to follow the same major as an undergraduate.

The first member of her family I ever met was her brother, and it was nerve-racking. Like meeting Superman. I'd heard a lot about this guy Grant, and knew how much he meant to Jill. I'd also seen pictures of him, and he was disturbingly handsome. You wouldn't want to pose next to him in a photo because he made mortal men look like garden gnomes.

He could have pulled the tough guy routine on me. He could have squeezed my hand harder than was comfortable to make sure I knew who was the bigger man. (It was he, the bodybuilder, by a lot.) But he didn't pull any of that macho nonsense. After all those years looking after his sister, maybe he could tell when he met someone who intended to do the same.

Jill's a sweetheart, soft-spoken and kind. She's also itty-bitty, standing just five feet tall, although . . . okay, let's just *give* her that one. On her chest, starting just a few inches below her neck, running vertically down, you can see the scar from her surgery, like a dry riverbed viewed from an airplane. Her heartbeat still has a murmur, and she goes for routine cardiology checkups, but otherwise, she's fine. She has given birth to two healthy babies. Our oldest daughter, now six, is named Audrey.

We chose that name during one of our sonogram sessions, when the doctor let us listen to this baby-to-be's nascent heart and told us it was perfect.

I knew Audrey would grow up having one of the

coolest uncles in the world, since he was already the greatest big brother in the world, not just to Jill but to me, too.

About a year before our little girl was born, my wife and I started calling Grant by a new nickname: Iron Man.

This was summer of 2008, and Marvel Studios had kicked off its cinematic universe with a new film starring Robert Downey Jr., and as soon as we walked out of the theater, my wife and I turned to each other.

"Did he remind you of . . . ?"

We called Grant immediately. It was a comparison he was happy to embrace.

The thing is, Grant not only looked like Robert Downey Jr., he acted like him. The charming wiseass routine, the paradoxical self-deprecating cockiness, the billion-dollar smile that beckoned you to join him on whatever mischief or caper he intended to perpetrate. Grant was fond of making blisteringly rude asides, then turning to the person who seemed to be most shocked and asking, "Oh my god, why would you *say* that?"

Grant was the blue-collar version of the billionaire playboy philanthropist.

In his twenties and early thirties, he had worked as a bartender at a pool hall, which made him a confidante and caregiver to a hell of a lot of people in both their happiest and darkest times—and most of them never forgot it. He seemed to be friends with everyone, and his future wife, Michelle, who came to Arizona from Illinois, quickly got to know everyone in Tucson simply by visiting a bar, a Trader Joe's, a church, or anywhere in that city with Grant Piontek at her side. He was the type of person who made friends everywhere and kept them forever.

But the charm thing . . . I can't overstate this. He later took a job as a corporate trainer with Golden Eagle, a local Budweiser distributor, but he was such a charismatic representative of the brand (and easy on the eyes) that they started using him as *a model in advertisements*. He was up on billboards. All over town. That flawless smile. Surrounded by people having fun. The King of Beers.

Jill and I settled in Los Angeles, where I found work as a reporter, and she pursued her career as a librarian. I write about movies for a living, and Grant always wanted to know the latest on whatever comic book adaptation was in the works. When we'd come back to visit Tucson, hitting the town with Grant was like hanging out with a real celebrity. You could see what a lifetime of goodwill had built for him. Grant looked out for everyone. And everyone returned the favor.

He was the Tony Stark of Tucson. Except, Grant didn't have a bad heart.

That's what we thought.

"Anthony, are you with Jill?"

Kelli's husband was on the phone. A cool October morning in 2009. Audrey was a little over one month old and Jill was about to leave home with her for a routine checkup with the pediatrician.

"Hold on," I said. "I'll go get her."

"Don't," he said. "Get somewhere she can't hear."

This was weird. This was wrong. I walked into the backyard, out of earshot.

Grant had a heart attack, I was told.

I remember saying *What?* over and over again, not from shock but pure disbelief. Those words simply made no sense. The next few words didn't either.

"He's gone."

He's gone.

It's still hard to believe, more than six years later. Grant can't be gone. Superheroes fall, but they always get up.

Grant was the portrait of physical fitness, and he was only thirty-eight years old. People in perfect health who are that young don't die unexpectedly. They just don't.

Except . . . it happened. It happened to him. It happened to us, his family. Again. Another child gone.

In the months before, Grant had told his mother, Patty, that he was thinking of going to the doctor. He was having weird chest pains, but maybe it was just a pulled muscle. He wasn't sure. My mother-in-law urged him to get checked out immediately, but Grant let it go. If it had been Jill or Kelli, they may have rushed to the emergency room, but Grant was never the one with the bad heart. That particular ailment had passed him by.

Then one day he said good-bye to Michelle and headed north to Flagstaff for a work conference, but on the morning of his presentation, Grant was a no-show. He wasn't answering any calls or texts either. They went to his hotel room, and there was no answer.

The evening before, Grant had excused himself early from dinner with his colleagues, saying he was feeling unusually tired. No one knew it then, but part of his heart had begun to tear just slightly. Basically, a leak breaks through, then the dam blows. Stats say 40 percent of people die instantaneously from aortic dissection. That's what we believe happened to Grant.

For all his life, he was the strong one. But when that hidden flaw inside finally gave way, it was catastrophic. There was no surviving.

Jill's heart, her actual heart, is still strong. But the thing inside us we call by that term, the thing that loves and aches and yearns . . . it hasn't been the same since.

When they were kids, superheroes were an armor Grant threw around Jill to make her feel brave, to make her feel powerful. But really, he was the armor. His strength became her strength. So when I think of Grant, I think of Iron Man. And when I think of Iron Man, I think of Tony Stark's heart, always just a fragment away from stopping forever.

Whenever a new Marvel movie comes out with Robert Downey Jr. as the character, my wife watches him onscreen with a smile on her face and tears in her eyes. Every wisecrack of Stark's leads to a laugh and pang of sorrow. When our son was born in 2013, *Iron Man 3* was his first movie. Ultron and Thanos themselves couldn't have stopped her from packing up our two-month-old little boy and hustling him to a Mommy and Me screening.

It's not Grant up there onscreen, of course, but . . . it feels like him. Same wiseass remarks. Same devilish charm. Same self-effacing nobility. And Jill knows her big brother would want to be sitting in that theater alongside her, watching one of their favorite heroes fight the good fight.

After Grant's funeral, my wife and I sat on a bed in her sister's house and tried to figure out what to do next. There was no changing what happened. Heroes always resurrect in the comics, but not in the real world. So how do you move forward when such a big part of your life is gone?

"We have to live twice as hard," I suggested. "Because he can't. We have to make the most of our time, out of the years he was cheated." And we've tried to do that, tried not to waste what we've been given. We've tried to remember what he stood for, and stand for those things. We tell our kids this, too.

There's a crack in our armor, and no fixing it. But Iron Man is proof that even broken hearts can still beat strong.

Maybe strongest of all.

THE WEIGHT OF FOUR-COLOR JUSTICE

CHRISTOPHER GOLDEN

I t's quiet in my house tonight. One son is at college and the other is at a concert with a lovely girl he's been seeing. My daughter has a virus—high fever—and she's out like a light for now, but I know she'll wake later. She's had a tough time with viruses since she was a baby and her fever went so high that she stopped breathing. Briefly, but it happened. She was in my wife's arms and I was out buying baby Tylenol to try to combat the fever. I came home to paramedics and a frantic family, but the baby was all right.

It's quiet in my house tonight. My wife is sleeping beside me as I type this. *Blue Bloods* is on the television set. She finds the show comforting for some reason, likes to fall asleep with it in the background.

It's quiet in my house tonight and I'm doing something I've never done before. I'm lying in bed with my laptop in the dark (well, except for the glows from the TV and my laptop screen). Maybe I'm writing this here quietly, because it feels more intimate, more confessional, like a journal. That's good . . . helpful. It's not like me to let people see too deep. I open up sometimes, sure; and on those rare occasions when I get torn up by grief, the emotions have to come out. Who can hide their pain under such circumstances? For the most part, though, things tend to stay down in the cellar of my mind . . . the place I put all the things I want to forget or that just don't bear thinking about. I mean, we all have a lot of unpleasant stuff in our past that just *is*, the stuff we can't do anything to change, and so what's the point of letting it under your skin?

That's been my MO all my life, I think. Even as a kid, I was always poking my nose into my friends' business, trying to help them solve their problems. Some of them took to calling me Quincy, after the old *Quincy, M.E.* TV series with Jack Klugman, because when someone I cared about was troubled, I felt like I had to be involved.

Just tonight, for the first time, it occurred to me that maybe the reason I wanted to solve everyone else's problems is that there wasn't anything I could do about my own.

It's quiet in my house tonight.

It's wonderful, that quiet.

My wife always says that men are simple creatures, that we really only need three things to be happy: food in the belly, peace in the home, and "the other thing." As much as I value the first and third, it's that middle one that means the most to me.

Peace in the home.

Let me back up. . . .

I don't remember my first comic book and I have a hard time believing most of the people who say they do. Could be just the way my memory works, of course. I'm terrible with chronology. When I was sick, my mother would bring me comics from the pharmacy, everything from *Richie Rich* to *Justice League of America*. Sometimes we'd visit my uncle's house in Gloucester and I would go through the wooden box full of old twelve-cent comics that sat there for years. I always enjoyed them, but at some point, they just *took*. The hook was in. I'd beg to go to the pharmacy with my mother so I could sift through the latest issues, or ride my bike down to Travis Drug in Framingham Center to check out the spinner racks there. When my brother and I stayed with my grandmother, we begged for her to stop at MacKinnon Drug in Sudbury.

We were Marvel kids, my brother Jamie and I. Sure, we liked DC well enough, but when we had a choice it was always Marvel Comics that we'd buy. He preferred Spider-Man and the Hulk, while my favorites were Daredevil and the X-Men, and we both loved the Marvel horror comics like *The Tomb of Dracula* and *Werewolf by Night*. While I don't remember the first comic book I ever read, *Tomb of Dracula* 15 was the first issue I ever bought for myself.

God, how I loved them. We used to take out our boxes of comics and organize them, just to look at them. We had the Mego Marvel action figures with their cloth and plastic costumes and built giant bases for them out of cardboard boxes. I still remember being in a toy store with my mother, pleading for those dolls. Yeah, no argument from me: they were dolls.

My mother indulged our love for superheroes, bought us whatever comics she could afford. I figure that, consciously or unconsciously, she knew we needed them. My father, on the other hand, never spent a moment thinking about what my brother and sister and I might need or want. He was Peter Pan, never growing up; and while I do believe he loved us, he was forever focused outward, away from the family.

To meet my father was to be charmed by him. The eldest of seven children, as a young man he might be sent out for a loaf of bread in the morning and not return until late afternoon, having stopped to see friends or girlfriends all through the day. Sort of adorable . . . until you consider that his mother had sent him out for that bread and she and his younger siblings were waiting for him at home. He carried that behavior forward throughout his life, a seed that blossomed into an unbreakable pattern. Entertaining himself was his only goal. Marital fidelity was a foreign country he perceived as inhospitable, and alcohol was his most trusted friend.

I loved my father and I still miss him. When he was around, he was wonderful company. He made pancakes on Saturday mornings and sometimes cooked "dragon tongues" (fried bologna) at lunch. He could be a total goofball, loved movies and books, and seemed to have friends everywhere. Whenever he had a hole in one of his T-shirts, my brother and I would jump on him and tear the shirt apart like small animals, and he would laugh. He took me to the circus, let me sit at his office desk . . . and he typed up my first short story for me. . . . I remember that he was proud. Though he was a terrible husband, he was a great dad . . . when he was around.

Trouble was, he wasn't around very often. Sure, our parents took us to the beach and we'd spend time in Maine or on Cape Cod during the summer, but far too often he was just . . . gone. Usually he was out with women other than my mother, but just as often, I think, he was drinking with his cronies in Boston politics. At some point, my mother couldn't take it anymore and they separated. They divorced when I was eleven years old and after that we saw him less and less.

If he set any example, it was a poor one. I had other father figures in my life, but of course none of them were my dad, and my actual father's behavior did nothing to teach me right from wrong. He taught me how to shave, but never thought a moment about what he might be teaching me about being a man or a husband, about being a responsible member of my community.

I learned those things from Captain America.

From Iron Man.

From Spider-Man.

From Ben Grimm and Reed Richards of the Fantastic Four.

Captain America seemed so sure of himself, so certain of the righteousness of his beliefs. He never hesitated to leap in to defend those who could not defend themselves. Iron Man had flaws, of course—he was an alcoholic, like my father—but he championed the use of both wealth and science for the betterment of humanity. Spider-Man taught us all that "with great power comes great responsibility," but I knew the comics weren't just talking about *super*powers. It seemed clear to me that simply having the upper hand—physically, intellectually, financially—gave a person the moral responsibility to intervene on behalf of others. Ben Grimm, aka the Thing, taught me that power and bluster and outward ugliness could hide the kindest hearts, and that people who seem abrasive and angry are often angry with themselves or their lot in life. Reed Richards—the Fantastic Four's so-called Mister Fantastic—taught me that even the most intelligent people needed to be grounded, that sometimes they needed to be reminded about what really mattered . . . the people they loved.

Marvel superheroes taught me right from wrong.

I don't think my mother had any idea that the comics she brought home, the four-color heroes I begged her for, would have such an impact on me; but at a time when I desperately needed positive models of male behavior, she provided them in bright stacks, thirty-two pages at a time. Comics gave me what my father could not—a clearly defined moral code and a sense of urgency about helping others and righting wrongs and standing up for what I believed in.

These role models were a gift . . . up to a point.

I defended my friends and did my best to be kind. I wanted my home to be a safe haven, so if any of them were having troubles they had somewhere to go, someone who would listen. I certainly wasn't perfect—I said and did things I regretted almost instantly, and if not instantly, then soon enough—but I strove to live up to the examples that my subconscious had absorbed from comics.

Those examples helped me in many ways—I offered those around me a shoulder to lean on, or to cry on, and an ally in difficult times—but they hurt me, too. I could be insufferably self-righteous. I knew better than everyone else and I interfered, sticking my nose in where it didn't belong. Comic book justice had given me a totally unrealistic, black-and-white view of right and wrong and the sense that I had to stand up for that view, to preach it to others.

It was during my junior year of college that I began to realize my idea of helping might sometimes be hurting those I loved. A close friend was having difficulty with her boyfriend and I made pronouncements about his behavior, her behavior, and what she ought to do next. She disagreed and grew furious with me for my condescending tone and for always stating things in a way that suggested I believed that only my opinion could ever have merit.

I confess this shocked and hurt me. Didn't she realize I only wanted to help, that I only wanted her to behave logically and lessen her emotional pain? We argued, of course, but over time I came to realize that she was right, that I had been less interested in listening and offering sympathy than I was in passing judgment. I behaved with the self-righteousness of the 1970's-era Captain America, when I was just some kid who'd invested too much faith in the soapbox morality of comic books. At the time, it was the only way I knew how to be a friend.

I still do this. When a friend is troubled or having difficulties in life, my first instinct is to help . . . or better yet, *fix* the problem for them. Of course, most of the time, people don't want us to fix their problems . . . just listen and reassure them. I like to believe that over the years I've learned to listen more and judge less, to sense when advice is welcome and when it is a nuisance.

Sometimes I fail at this, but I try.

My father died of cancer at the age of fifty-four, a few weeks before my twentieth birthday.

It's quiet in my house tonight, and I still miss my father. When Bobby Simone died on *NYPD Blue* and all the characters trooped in and out to say their farewells to him, I wept. When I saw *Big Fish* in the movie theater, about the young writer whose relationship with his father is so reminiscent of my own experience, I cried silently and uncontrollably as the credits rolled.

My whole life, people have told me that I look like him and share many of his mannerisms. These moments are bittersweet. He had some wonderful qualities, but I always promised myself that I would never be like my father. I fought so hard to be a better man than he was, subjected myself to a totally impossible standard, and had unrealistic expectations of others . . . and of myself. I've learned that I'm not a superhero, not some righteous fictional man who can do no wrong. When I've hurt and disappointed people, as we all do at times, I have been gutted by my disappointment with myself. I've been forgiven by others far sooner than I could forgive myself.

Comics have changed a lot since I was a kid. With every passing year, heroes are more flawed, more fallible, and I believe that's for the best. There are lost children everywhere who are looking for role models, and it's better for them to see examples of people who sometimes fail but who always get up, dust themselves off, and keep trying their best.

It's quiet in my house tonight. Times like this, I always think of myself as a sentry and protector, standing guard over my sleeping family. . . .

Captain America and his friends taught me well. Sometimes too well. It took life and death to teach me a much more important lesson.

We are all only human.

SUPERHEROES AND LOVE

DAREDEVIL, ELEKTRA, AND THE NINJA WHO STOLE MY VIRGINITY

JAMIE FORD

Half of you will love this.

As you read along you will undoubtedly nod your head in agreement, feeling every embarrassing turn taken by a fool in love. You'll look into these pages of pulped wood and vegetable-based black ink and see your own steely reflection, because you—yes, *you*—will have either been there, broken heart in hand, or will have come perilously close enough to recognize the folly. You'll see this yarn as a cautionary tale, the kind where you can laugh nervously at the protagonist (yours truly) and hope to God, Allah, Buddha, Richard Dawkins, or whichever deity you align yourself with and say, "What kind of corner liquor store hooch did Cupid poison his arrows with before he shot them into the heart of *this* poor sucker, and how the heck do I avoid the same ill fate?"

Then there's the other half.

You, the nonfeelers—those quantitative souls who

measure love using a slide rule or perhaps a graphing calculator—who make lists of the pros and cons about whether you should marry someone, instead of throwing caution and rational thought to the wind and falling madly into the murky, stygian undertows of love.

If you find yourself in this *other* category, I suggest you flip to the next essay, or reread the previous one, because what follows is a tale that includes old friends, old flames, broken hearts, Daredevil and Elektra as ill-fated star-crossed lovers, and lots of running with sharp, pointy objects.

Oh, and also included is a brief moment of awkward teenage sex.

This, my dear friends, is a confession and an exploration about those people in our lives who are like Halley's comet. They come around once or, if we're lucky, twice in a lifetime and, when they do, they affect our gravity. Sometimes they're a wishing star on a dark night. Other times they are a rogue black hole, unseen until it's too late and suddenly they're sucking up your atmosphere like milk from the bottom of a cereal bowl.

For yours truly, this person was named Allison.*

And whether she was the former or the latter, I'll let you decide. After all, time and space—and for that part, reality itself—can only truly be judged from the vantage point of an uninvolved third party.

---

* And, yes, I do realize that in a certain prime-time television sitcom years ago, there was a beguiling and entropic girlfriend also named Allison, but please, dear reader, don't let that prejudice you—not yet anyway.

My particular Allison was that quintessential first crush turned girlfriend, the one who made my palms sweat, my voice crack, and who carbonated my sixteen-year-old hormones in a way that turned an already awkward teenage boy into a blubbering, guffawing mass of nervousness and early masturbatory daydreaming.

She was everything a geeky, comic book–collecting, Dungeons & Dragons–playing lad could dream of—long auburn hair (the color of a unicorn's mane), a ravishing smile (I think she wore braces to make her teeth seem *less* perfect), caramel eyes (that was the rumor anyway; most boys fell into a hypnotic trance when they dared to make eye contact and woke, days later in a state of amnesia), and a natural charisma of 18 (no saving roll versus charm person spell), and best of all, she worked as a teacher's assistant in the chem lab. She was the living, breathing embodiment of every Journey song ever written (including the Steve Perry song "Don't Fight It"—the duo with Kenny Loggins ☺ ha!) and every single one of my friends was in love with her. Looking back, the sheer amount of chemistry books we collectively borrowed just to be perspiring in her presence was . . . was . . . *encyclopaedian*.

But of all of us, the few, the proud, the acne-scarred troglodytes who spent every lunch in the chem lab fawning over this Minerva—this virgin goddess of art, poetry, and the Periodic Table of Elements, I, your humble narrator, was the one who finally asked her out.

After months of pining away for this impossible girl

(I say "pining" you say "stalking" . . . you say "to-MAY-to", I say, "to-MAH-to" . . . let's not muddy the water with facts) she finally relented and agreed to go with me to the winter formal. Rumors that I pretended to be dying and that I asked the Make-A-Wish Foundation to facilitate this date were merely rumors perpetuated by my jealous and heartbroken friends.

Now I must mention that the winter formal was *a big hurking deal* back in the Mesolithic Age in which I attended high school. Unlike today's Clearasil generation whose text-driven mating rituals resemble something like this:

> JAKE: hey
>
> KARISSA: wat up. watchn netflix
>
> JAKE: me too. Wanna hang out
>
> KARISSA: when
>
> JAKE: Saturday.
>
> KARISSA: U mean homecoming
>
> JAKE: yea
>
> KARISSA: lemme ask my mom.
>
> JAKE: ok
>
> KARISSA: ok. See you there I gess.
>
> JAKE: k. Bye.
>
> (Note: the only punctuation in this conversation was added by autocorrect.)

You see, *back in my day* (I feel geriatric just by using that phrase) not only did young men have to actually *ask* a girl out—they had to do it with style. In my case,

I sent my dear crush a stuffed bear and a series of notes, each written in a different language: German, Italian, Spanish, French, and finally English (and I translated these *by hand* using actual foreign language dictionaries checked out from the public library).

Plus the dance/date itself involved corsages and tuxedos and dinner reservations and the borrowing (and cleaning and vacuuming) of a car. To say nothing of the actual event itself, which was Victorian in decorum compared to today's dances where kids snort a tenth of molly in the parking lot only to *get their grind on* for a few minutes before leaving to hook up someplace more convenient than romantic—to paraphrase a line from Mitch Hedberg: "Ohhhh, baby, I love you so much. This is our song. Do you remember our special night, when I fucked you at the pet cemetery?"

So off we went.

Our date was akin to a Norman Rockwell painting of all-American splendor that ended with a walk to her doorstep and that first innocent kiss in the moonlight (with braces—not quite so magical in retrospect, but I was *sixteen* and had never had more than an imaginary girlfriend so gimme a break, pal!).

I remember driving home in the Seattle rain, rolling down my window, and shouting at the night as though I were Sir Edmund Hillary having just conquered Mount Everest. The evening was beatific, transcendent, and the smile on my face so epically permanent that when I went to my job as a busboy at a seafood restaurant the next day, the salty old waitresses got together and collectively decided that I had lost my virginity.

But . . . it was just a kiss. And sometimes, a kiss is more than a kiss.

Which brings us to Daredevil and Elektra.

Frank Miller's run on *Daredevil* as artist and writer was revolutionary in bringing deep, brooding crime noir to the comic medium. No longer was Daredevil a wise-cracking, crime-fighting buffoon—he matured, he grew up and haunted a pre-Giuliani NYC landscape rife with muggers, hookers, crackheads, and the occasional crime lord.

But more important, Miller also introduced readers to the heart-rending madness of noble romantic tragedy with the inclusion of Elektra—a one-off character who was to be nothing more than an amuse-bouche in a filler story but who would later become one of the most memorable and tragic antiheroines of the twentieth century.

Elektra Natchios, the wealthy, privileged daughter of Greece's ambassador to the United States who, as a college student at New York's Columbia University, and surrounded by bodyguards, falls in love with Daredevil's alter ego, Matt Murdock (gotta love Stan Lee's penchant for alliteration: Matt Murdock, Peter Parker, Reed Richards, Stephen Strange, Otto Octavius, and J. Jonah Jameson, to say nothing of Fin Fang Foom—the dragon who wore pants. Ah, but I daringly digress).

Matt Murdock is the blue-collar son of a washed-up prizefighter who is later murdered in the streets of Hell's

Kitchen. Plus, Matt is blind. Sure, he has heightened senses and a type of radar that allows him to fight crime as Daredevil, but to the normal world, he's less than a regular Joe—certainly to Elektra's complicated, upper-crust family he's a nobody. Yet before you know it, they are sharing their innermost secrets.

What happens next is pure romantic tragedy worthy of Shakespeare if the great Bard of Avon included ninjas, because terrorists arrive in NYC to kidnap Elektra's father, and when Matt (Daredevil) tries to intervene . . . her father is killed in the melee. Blaming Matt, Elektra leaves the country, only to return decades later as a cold, seemingly heartless, trained mercenary who takes what she wants and kills those she must. And, of course, she's destined to cross paths with our horned hero.

Elektra the student and wealthy scion returns as Elektra the *assassin*. (Frank Miller modeled her after the body-builder Lisa Lyon, whose physique was immortalized by the likes of Richard Avedon and Robert Mapplethorpe, but to me, the perfect Elektra would have been the young French actress Carole Bouquet.)

(Go ahead and google her, I'll wait.)

Waiting

Like in the James Bond film *For Your Eyes Only*, where Bouquet plays the assassin Melina Havelock, and says, "I don't expect you to understand. You're English, but I'm half Greek. And Greek women, like *Elektra*, always avenge their loved ones," our Elektra comes back seeking vengeance and is ultimately hired to kill Daredevil—

though a part of her still loves the man behind the mask.

And he, of course, still loves her—despite being in a relationship with another woman. (See, Frank Miller really kicked it up a notch.)

Meanwhile, back in my boyish, teenage, Sony Walkman–wearing world, I was about to experience a similar circumstance of the heart, turned upside down, because my one-off date became a roaring, all-consuming first love. We made awkward angels in the snow on quiet winter nights. We snuck off to concerts her stepfather didn't approve of in the spring. And by summer we were a perpetual heartbeat away from *going all the way,* but with gentlemanly restraint, I insisted we wait, *because I loved her.* That sensitivity led to nights with her crying in my arms as she confessed the painful moments of her childhood. And by the next homecoming dance I'm Heathcliff and Allison is my Catherine, and tragedy waits in the wings for us both.

A fundamental problem that I didn't mention earlier (why ruin the magic) was that, like Daredevil, I was working-class poor. My favorite coat was a leather jacket from Goodwill that I bought for five bucks. Allison's family was wealthy, with a waterfront home, a condo in Hawaii, an enormous sailboat, and all the proper trappings of money and normalcy while I was eking out an existence with my single mother in a rent-controlled barrio on the bad side of town.

And like Elektra's father, Allison's paterfamilias was

an important person and a hulk of a human being. It was as though fate had conspired to create one of the most overprotective parents imaginable. He was a decorated marine and the only son, the eldest, with three younger sisters, who then married Betty Crocker and had four daughters, of which Allison was the oldest.

I'd like to say that he simply hated me, but that would cast him as a one-dimensional character and he was far more complex. He loved his daughters the way fat, balding, white guys adore bowling trophies. And when Allison was no longer content to sit on the shelf and be admired, her stepfather had a friend who worked as a deputy for the sheriff's department inform me that I was no longer welcome to date Allison.

It was like something out of a bad seventies movie. Except I didn't have a monkey sidekick or a wisecracking, truck-driving buddy with Snowman for a CB handle.

So while I'm reading Daredevil each month (and watching for flashing lights in my rearview mirror), I'm now *wishing* terrorists would kidnap Allison's stepfather, at least until senior prom. Because when we wouldn't stop seeing each other, she was forced to move out. She lived with friends, off and on, told me she loved me, but sobbed because she missed her family. She tried to stay away, tried to understand who she really was.

And as Elektra returned every so often to the pages of Daredevil to stoke the embers in the heart of a sightless hero, so did Allison return to me, rebelling against logic and the wishes of her stepfather, feeding the hopes of blind, ruinous, teenage love. But after seeing the familial destruction occurring between Allison and her parents, and believing the hardest choices in life aren't between what's right and what's wrong but between what's right and what's best—I chose to break my own heart and walk away.

And as much as she respected my noble gesture, she never forgave me.

The emptiness hardened her and chaos followed, because now she rebelled against her stepfather *and* me. Now she recklessly dated whom she wanted (including my best friend), when she wanted (on our silly high school anniversary), and she left me in an emotional junk heap, coming back, picking me up when she was bored and needed something akin to love and tossing me aside when she had discovered a new toy. And I fell for it . . . *every . . . stinking . . . time*, until college mercifully took us in separate directions and I was free from this toxic, crazy, drama-filled relationship that I'd helped create.

I didn't see Allison again until after I had followed months of Frank Miller's Elektra saga to its fateful conclusion—with Elektra defeating Daredevil only to die at the hands of his archnemesis, Bullseye. I can still see those pages, the blood drawn in stark black ink as Elektra staggers back to the doorstep of the only man she has ever cared for and dies in his arms. And even after she's buried, Matt Murdock goes mad, insane with grief—literally exhuming her body and cradling her corpse because he can't believe that she's truly gone. It was the most heartbreaking moment I'd ever read.

Almost as heartbreaking as the journal I kept my first year in art school.

There's an entry that reads:

Allison showed up unexpectedly. How she tracked down my dorm room at Seattle U is a mystery. She showed up about nine in the morning, holding the bear I'd given her for homecoming. She met my roommate, Alan, as he was leaving and made herself at home. I stayed behind, cut class to "talk" and that talk involved her sleeping with me—as in, going all the way (finally), which was exciting but also disappointing because I know she wasn't with me because of anything permanent like LOVE. Not anymore. She was here because she needed me for the moment and in that moment she could take what she wanted from this foolish eighteen-year-old virgin. It was like I was something she had forgotten to take care of and once she had crossed me off her list, she left.

I don't expect her to call, but I still love her. Fucking stupid, I know. And like a bad penny, I have a feeling she's going to keep reappearing, showing up on my doorstep, tapping on my window, being on the other end of a wrong-number phone call in the middle of the night, silent before hanging up. I wish I could stop answering the phone. I guess tomorrow I'll begin counting the days until I don't think of her anymore.

My next class was Life Drawing 101. I sat with my pencil and sketch pad and regarded the nude figure of a middle-aged model. I was forced to draw a naked stranger's timeworn curves for three hours, while also drawing mental conclusions about Allison. About awkward, emotionally confounding sex, about anticlimactic climaxes, brief in pleasure, the emptiness afterward seemed never ending. Sleeping with Allison had been as easy as falling down a steep hill and left just as many bruises and internal injuries.

Despite other dates and the occasional girlfriend, it took about a year for a single, placid day to pass when I didn't think, brood, fret, or otherwise long for Allison. I remember sitting at the bus stop, realizing that two days had miraculously passed, and then a week, and now years will go by.

But back then, it wasn't quite so simple.

When Elektra died in the arms of Daredevil and in the pages of Marvel, her creator, Frank Miller, was promised that she would never be brought back in the traditional sense. (She did come back to life a year later, oddly enough, in a Miller story line where she is revived and lives a monkish existence away from the material, emotional world—she's found peace, alone, and Daredevil doesn't know she exists, and *that's* the ending Frank Miller intended.)

But sadly, promises between editors and writers are weak paper when private companies go public and Elektra is no longer seen as a heartbreaking character in the canon of graphic literature but as an asset, a piece of intellectual property that needs to be dusted off and used for profit. She's like a zombie (and in one case, an actual zombie!) who keeps coming back in the hands of other creators, artists, and storytellers.

And Allison, my Elektra, kept coming back as well.

She would appear via random calls, cards, and letters, all with a very clear subtext, thinly disguised. (I'm embarrassed to say that I gave in once or twice, *so I won't say it*.) But eventually I resisted. And fate persisted. After college I had relocated to the suburbs of Seattle, moved into an apartment with a roommate, and was trying to start my career in the newspaper biz, when walking to a row of mailboxes, whom do I run into? Yes, Allison had been living in the very same apartment complex. Uncomfortable moment? Why, yes, indeed. *Fate, you are a fickle, teasing bastard and I will get you, my little pretty, and your damned dog, Toto, too!*

I remember expecting to step backward into a bear trap and then Allison would mouth Elektra's words: "Be grateful that I did not set that trap to sever your foot. I would have—but then, you would not be so completely immobilized. So utterly helpless . . ."

And then I'd wake up, buried beneath a pile of rubble. Barely breathing.

But instead, I said good-bye. I passed the test. And years passed in that moment.

Twenty years.

And when I finally came to my senses, I found myself in a very unhappy marriage (my fault, for running *from* someone instead of running *to* someone). I was still reading comics and still fumbling around with this thing called fiction. And I got a call, out of the great blue yonder, from my Elektra. She wasn't dead after all. She was alive and well and wishing to see me—the married her, wanting to see the married me, at our twenty-year high school reunion.

Honestly, it was nice to hear her voice, to apologize for my lack of maturity all those years ago. But most of all, it was nice to share that I'd be going to a writer's conference instead. I told her that I had no interest in rewriting the past and that novels were more interesting to me than exploring nonfiction. But I wished her well.

And I thought that was the end.

Little did I know that a few years later, while on tour for my first novel—a surprise sleeper hit about long-lost love—I would find myself standing at a lectern in an auditorium in Poulsbo, Washington, speaking to a crowd of three hundred people.

I did my thing as authors do—offering one part entertainment, one part literary vaudeville, and one part jumping up and down on Oprah's couch. And then someone in the audience asked about my first love—my high school sweetheart (my Elektra).

I hesitated.

I drew a very deep breath.

And then I shared a brief story about Allison, albeit a stridently self-deprecating one, and as I was telling this tale of awkward first kisses with braces and lasting heartache and growing up, I looked out into the audience and the great and terrible *She*—Allison—was sitting in the middle row, about halfway up, staring back at me.

I hadn't seen her since I was nineteen years old, though I'd felt her in my heart on occasion. She looked the same—older of course, more mileage, but the same. And I watched as she put her hand to her lips and smiled and laughed and nodded.

Then fingers snapped. The audience was clapping as I was being escorted to the table where I'd sign books for an hour, patiently waiting for a reunion that I had never imagined—not in a million authorly lifetimes—but she never showed.

Like Elektra, Allison had become skilled in the fine art of deception.

She vanished.

And I was left wondering if she was ever there at all.

EVERYTHING I KNOW ABOUT LOVE, I LEARNED FROM GAMBIT AND ROGUE

KARINA COOPER

For most of my life, I never really identified with your standard superheroes. I respected them, certainly—Wonder Woman was always awesome because she could stand equal to any hero *and* she was a girl, Superman was pretty cool because *eye lasers* and invulnerability, and Batman *really* liked his toys.

They were fun. Strong. Colorful. But if you'd asked me, I couldn't say that I really got what they were. *Who* they were, specifically in regards to what and who I was. Those legends were out of my reach—gods among kings, entertaining and full of adventure, but never mine to associate with. They just didn't speak to me.

Which was fine, because I was pretty sure I didn't need a superhero to save my life.

Contrary to popular belief, turns out superheroes can work in mysterious ways. Whatever I thought, life conspired to make sure I tripped over the one that I needed when I needed her most.

My family consisted of a single mother and a brother thirteen months older than me. When we were teeny, I'm told, my brother and I got along like a house on fire—which I understand means something like "great." As we got older, we got along like you'd imagine a house on fire *actually* feels like. As in, mass destruction.

In between bouts of full-scale war, my brother taught me the awesomeness of Transformers—original die-cast metal figures, naturally. I played with dolls like any other girl was expected to, but I also played with GI Joes, with Starscream (I actually *liked* his voice), and with Teenage Mutant Ninja Turtles. I loved Donatello best. During that point in time when our interests overlapped—and my brother wasn't so keen to abandon me for playmates of his own—we watched cartoons. Around 1989 when it aired, we watched the original animated X-Men, *Pryde of the X-Men*.

I was seven years old. Too young to think that I'd need a superhero someday but old enough to act like a sponge for a one-shot cartoon. In a quiet, long-term way, this minuscule act of generosity on my brother's part set the foundation for the rest of my life—or at least, as the X-Men tend to have it, *this* life in *this* continuity. (In other continuities, *I'm* the superhero.)

My mother tried her best for us in those days, but it's hard for a single mom raising two kids on a nine-to-five—especially in San Francisco. She worked a lot, and though I've never had the courage to ask, I think she played a lot, too. I wouldn't blame her. Mom had us fairly young, and now that I'm without children in my thir-ties, I can't imagine how hard it was to raise two toddlers by herself while still in her twenties.

At that time, we were too small to look after ourselves, so she hired a babysitter, a married mother with two teenagers of her own—a boy and a girl. Since our baby-sitter had her own family to take care of, the couple watched us in their home, took care of us when we got the chicken pox, and made sure we had good food to eat and a place to stay.

We stayed a lot. Sometimes, we stayed the night.

Sometimes, I woke up in the shared bed sobbing.

Those were the memories that surfaced first.

We moved a few times after California. By the time we settled in Virginia, I'd gotten used to coming home after school by myself. My older brother was supposed to be the responsible one, but he was already a troublemaker and spent as much time outside playing with friends as he could. Sometimes, he stuck around. Mostly, he kept to himself. Mom didn't believe in things like Nintendo, see, and all our friends did.

The closest my brother and I got to bonding in those days was over Saturday morning cartoons. Though we usually argued over who would watch what, we settled easily on *X-Men: The Animated Series*. I met Gambit and Rogue for the first time.

I only sort of understood her whole "no touch" issue—

people who touched her dropped into comas. Seemed like a good reason not to touch her, didn't it? The awareness for what that meant for Rogue, the compassion for how that kind of isolation shaped her, didn't come to me until later.

Saturday morning was special—a place and time entirely disconnected from the rest. Reality was different.

When Mom eventually brought home her fiancé, I was well into a comfortable routine of independence. I didn't need or want someone around messing it all up. I didn't like the new guy, I didn't like that he came with kids of his own, and I especially didn't like how scared those kids made me feel. Opening up to my new stepsister in the only way I knew how didn't get the best results—she felt I was copying her every move, and I just wanted to be liked by the older sister I'd never had. Every time she lashed out at me, I tried harder to be someone she'd like.

Someone, for example, like herself.

This cycle didn't end well.

Take the sudden appearance of a father figure and mix it with the nightmare that is puberty, add the hellish landscape of public school for extra fun, and I was ripe for the first escapist avenue that came my way. I will forever be grateful that it came in the form of books. When my world became too much to handle alone, I always had a way out. Even if only for a little while.

* * *

Some years later, and I was officially classified as an odd kid—always reading, never entirely focused on anything *real*. I'd already grown wary of love; in fact, I'd become downright cynical—a sort of world-weariness that masqueraded as practicality when it was really exhaustion and fear.

I often joke that I'm the most balanced one in the family, and this humor covers a lot. I don't remember when my mother started coming to me with her grown-up troubles, but I became something of a therapist along the way. I think that because I was practical, it was mistaken for maturity. It made it harder for me to open up—I picked up too much knowledge that wasn't mine. By the time I was thirteen, I'd developed Rogue's reaction to people in general: if they got too close, I took on their baggage. I didn't know how to let it go.

The year I naively nursed a crush for a flesh and blood human—instead of the awkward pressure I felt to go through the motions like everyone else—things had devolved at home. My folks were always fighting, and my brother was constantly in trouble. I had discovered theater, which kept me away from the uneasy environment, too busy for the impromptu therapy sessions I was already tired of.

All that quality time onstage with the star of the show slipped in under my wariness and turned into full-blown puppy love.

It was the only time I *really* tried—the one time I thought it might be worth trying. The night my year-long crush finally asked me on a date, my mother wouldn't let me go. It was near the end of my freshman year, and I was already scraped raw from peer pressure and hormones and the sheer embarrassment of existing. I was always fighting with my stepfather, feuding with my stepsister, and trying to cover for my brother. I spent so long trying to be everything to everyone that I didn't know who I was. Only that for this night, I could be the girl asked out on a date by a guy she liked.

With one phone call, I was suddenly placed in the painfully embarrassing position of explaining that I couldn't go on a date because my mother and stepfather had gotten into a protracted domestic dispute.

How does a kid—no matter how mature she's forced to be—describe *that*? How does a child of fourteen explain that she was *so tired* and so embarrassed, that she was angry and didn't want to go home to deal with the drama? That she'd rather go on the date—her first *real* date—and sing Beatles songs and watch a play with him and stay out forever.

Short answer? I didn't try. Not really. I tore the Band-Aid off—announced the ugliness for what it was, right out in the open—and left the wound exposed to the air, painful and throbbing.

The boy awkwardly made his apologies. I can't say for sure what he thought, but he definitely had no idea how to proceed from there. Neither did I. I'd tried to touch someone, and gotten burned for my efforts. That was the end of my crush, and the end of any interest I had in going through that again.

Like the wary X-Man I met so long ago on a Saturday morning and all but forgotten in the interim, this moment hit me the same way Ms. Marvel's psyche hit Rogue—too much, too hard, and too painful. The event shaped the rest of her life, just as this one shaped mine.

When my mother and stepfather finally divorced, we moved away.

My cynicism only grew as the years went by. In North Carolina, I did everything I could to be a tomboy—too boyish for pretty, too mouthy for respectable. I hoped it would keep me from being noticed, pursued, or touched. I built the walls that would keep people from relating to me, or wanting to try. I buried myself in books and kept very few friends. I didn't trust anyone to "touch" me and not lose their mind—or worse, inject themselves too far into mine. When the adults in the rural community started teasing about marrying me off to "a nice military boy," I fled the state.

I was fifteen, going on sixteen, when Mom and I ended up back in a different part of Virginia. My brother stayed behind. Contrary to musical numbers, there were no strapping young lads lining up to escort me around a gazebo while singing about how much they loved me. Rightly so. Odd had turned into prickly; a sheet of armor as thick as my books now protected the exposed nerve that my inner voice had become.

I knew that I didn't want to be touched—not touched as in physically, not like a hand to my arm or a hug. The touching that Rogue feared began as a physical thing, but it was the consequences she hated most—the same consequences I carried. I didn't want someone else's thoughts in my head, disguised as memories. I didn't want their voices in my psyche.

I was desperately afraid of the people around me and the baggage they'd already forced me to carry.

I started to remember things. Little things at first, triggered by harmless nothings.

I recalled the awful feelings when I woke up sobbing in a bed that wasn't mine, and the dismissive laughter that accompanied it. Then I remembered how I'd get yanked through a room by my hair. Then came the hands that strayed where no hands should be laid on a child. The laughter when I successfully mimicked an act taught by a family that was supposed to be taking care of me. I had been eager to please, because what child doesn't want the praise of those around her?

I didn't tell anyone. I didn't quite believe myself. And even if it was true, so what? It was years ago. I was older. Independent. I was a teenager who'd learned how to repress memories that didn't suit the world I wanted to live in.

When my brother left us, it was simply the way it was. When my mother made choices that didn't include me, that was fine, too. I separated myself from everyone—present in physical form but emotionally detached. I already knew that I would never marry, have kids, or otherwise trust that someone would be there for me—much *less* forever.

I was broken inside, but I couldn't understand the fundamentals of *how*. Memories, guilt, a slow fury simmered inside me, scars from years of betrayal—right or wrong, and there was plenty of both.

All I could do, all I wanted to do, was live my life *alone*. But at fifteen years old (going on sixteen, and this was the age where that sort of thing mattered), I knew I couldn't just become a hermit. I needed money—to live on, to buy the things I wanted, and replace all the books I'd lost over the years of traveling light.

So I applied for a job at a comic shop. It looked like a cool place. I liked comics in passing and art in general and things I could call *mine* in specific, so I thought I'd give it a shot. It didn't even occur to me that I'd be the only girl working there—I barely even considered the fact that I was a girl with any depth of meaning. At that point, I was a sexless biped with long blond hair, stick limbs, and a habit of wearing my brother's old hand-me-downs.

Comics became my go to for short reads. They were perfect for break time adventures, bold and filled with life. They were as much of an escape as a way to pass the time, just like the books I loved.

I didn't know it then, but the comic shop that hired me helped save my life.

* * *

I honed my social skills because that's what retail does for you—you learn to put on a smile, to make like you're having a great day, to pretend the customer is the most important thing in the world. If you're lucky, you learned to enjoy it. Like Rogue in *X-Men*, I picked up the traits and habits of those I came into contact with. While hers was a genetic predisposition, mine was taught by hard experience—I adopted peoples' likes and dislikes, altered myself, and I did it all without any conscious effort.

As a social chameleon, my only *real* talent was dressing down into as inconspicuous a default template as possible. I developed a kind of armor—an invulnerability that made it so I could fly away from every moment anytime I wanted.

And like Rogue at her best, I pretended I was fine. Because it was abnormal, I hid the fact that I hated to be touched, to be *close*. All the while, deep inside, I was desperate to find even one person who could do it without screwing with my head any more than it already was. I was lonely, but I carried the secrets and voices and baggage of all the people who'd touched me prior and they echoed and reechoed until I learned that quiet moments were impossible to handle.

So I never stopped reading. When I started work at the comic store, I promptly enrolled in the employee hold plan. This ensured that most of what I made went right back into the store. A smart plan, and it made it easy to buy comics by the handful.

I started with comics whose art or concept I found appealing. I was drawn to fantastical worlds, like Avalon Studios' *Aria*. I returned to stories that had what we would call today an "urban fantasy feel"—gorgeous art with kick-ass women front and center, like Michael Turner's *Witchblade* and *Fathom*, or David Finch's *Ascension*.

The third corner in my growing foundation, the thing that would sync with old-school cartoons and a whim of a job, struck me by accident. While organizing the stacks, I stumbled across a special *X-Men* issue. I recalled that my brother liked *X-Men* (my brother, mind, because even then, there were all these rules about what gender was supposed to like which comics) and so I thought I'd be nice and pick it up for him. We weren't living together anymore, and at just turned sixteen, I figured I'd gain some cool points for being the sister that worked at a comics joint and slung a superhero comic his way.

Silver holographic foil embellished the title, and a blown-up action shot of Rogue and Gambit brawling across the cover promised all kinds of entertainment. She wore green and yellow spandex; he sported his unmistakable pink armored vest under a brown trench coat. It was classic *X-Men*, and even better, it had a full foldout cover for maximum impact.

Oh, yeah. I was racking up the points even *holding* this thing.

I couldn't just send it off to him, I needed to read it first—nothing crossed my field without getting read at least once. As it turned out, reading it was the best thing to happen to me—to me as I was then and to me as I am now—in a very long time.

The story took what I'd absorbed years earlier in the animated series and turned it into something raw and emotional—Rogue and Gambit, in love but at odds after an explosive kiss that left the smooth-talking Cajun in a coma and Rogue on the run. She was angry, manic, haunted. Trying to hide from something she didn't quite get, desperate to love somebody she couldn't trust. It wasn't about saving the world, it was about two broken, flawed people trying to make it *work*.

I touched that comic and took a piece of them with me. Seared both superheroes into my mind and my heart, and if my subconscious stapled that special anniversary edition over my fraying armor, well, that was okay, too. In the pages of that comic, the thing I'd picked up on a whim for a brother I hadn't seen in months, I found something I hadn't yet learned how to articulate: I found me.

Amusingly, the issue never did make it to my brother. While rifling through the two shoe boxes that hold what's left of my comics today, I found it nestled between a stray *10th Muse* and the first issue of Top Cow's *The*

Darkness/Batman. Its publication date is listed as October, 1995.

I was only thirteen when Marvel wrote the comic that set the bar for the rest of my life.

We moved again in July 1999. I was a couple months shy of seventeen. My mom was staying at her boyfriend's house, leaving me to my own devices. My invulnerability was impenetrable. So much so that when I dated a person, I did it with the kind of shallow motives that would make a dude brofist me if I were a man.

What I wanted, what people wanted from me, didn't matter. I'd scored up some geek cred in my years of online text-based roleplay, sessions of D&D around the table, and in my time as a comic book slinger; I strapped it all up into a surefire pillow fort that I felt like I could comfortably defend. I was a gamer. A nerd. A bookworm. I was a geek who hadn't yet figured out what being a girl meant, and wasn't all that inclined to worry about it.

But I didn't leave my bad habits behind. That power of Rogue's—of mine—remained. I absorbed the people around me, used them like plates in my armor, until even I didn't know who I was—it changed depending on who I was with. For a long time, that was okay.

I was seventeen going on thirty, with an open-door policy for friends in need of crash space and a weekly commitment to local LARPs. That's live action role-playing, for you uninitiated, and it's about as nerdy as sitting around pretending to be vampires and werewolves—except more, because we *actually* dressed up for it. As it turned out, it was another excuse to behave like someone I wasn't.

Among my fellow gamers, a twenty-two-year-old guy stood out—he was friends with friends of mine, a LARPer, and geeky enough that we became friends pretty quickly.

Shortly after, he moved back home across the state. We stayed in touch, the way I always stay in touch—online or nothing. That habit started early. The Internet is for porn, cats . . . and instant messaging.

He and I had a lot in common, including our love for text-based gaming, and a lot that we didn't agree on. Our debates were fierce and spirited. For the first time in a long time, I began to wonder how dangerous it'd be to touch someone—and with it, I worried over how badly it would mess me up. Too much, I figured. In that, Rogue was the braver of us—at least she'd kissed Gambit (even if they did think the world was ending).

I didn't want my world to end. I'd already gotten closer to this guy than I ever had to anyone else, and I could feel the voices altering inside my psyche—and that made me afraid. So I ran.

Frankly, I didn't handle it any better than Rogue in that anniversary issue. Somewhere along the way, he came to be my Remy, patiently and cautiously pursuing a woman who could very well wreck his world if he got too close—I was *that* volatile.

He didn't seem to care. He was persistent, and he was kind, and when I finally agreed to date him a year later, I made a backup plan. An escape route. I reserved a large portion of myself, sealed it off with the rationale that it was fine because he'd leave anyway—or I'd leave first. Rogue knew how to protect herself, see, how to keep from getting touched, and so did I. I believed that he'd see how messed up I was, see the demons I throttled back behind the armor, see how easily I absorbed people around me, and go running—and of course he would, because that's what real people *do*. Real people aren't comic book superheroes.

Real people don't kiss a girl, fall into a coma, wake up, and *still* patiently, persistently go after the girl they love. Most don't know how to handle a past scarred by trauma and abuse.

Superheroes save the world, and sometimes they save each other, but Rogue and Gambit? They'd never, *ever* work out in the real world. If I was Rogue, and he was Gambit, then the outcome was already determined.

I kept one foot out the door, ready to run at a moment's notice.

The first mix CD he gave me was called *For the Love of a Princess*. In faded color, he'd added artwork pulled from his favorite love story of all time—Remy and Rogue, casual attire, swept into the kind of kiss that swore to defy *everything* except the love they shared.

Okay, I thought, fingering the plastic case. *Maybe I could give this one a shot.*

I was eighteen going on blindsided.

Years later, the tale of Rogue and Gambit continues. They work it out—they stumble over something else that gets in the way. Sometimes, they get in their own way. They break it off—they find each other again. They save the world. And then they fall victim to their own fears all over again. Because that's what happens to superheroes.

It happens to us, too.

Over a decade later, and the man I eventually learned to trust—who spent years patiently unraveling those demons, the masks, the armor I'd cobbled together from the absorbed remains of the people I'd known—hasn't let me down. The going is tough, just as it is for Gambit and Rogue. The enemies we face aren't as dangerous to the world at large, but they are as real a threat to us as any supervillain. He gets the sharp side of my tongue more often than not, but he's got a quick wit of his own and a powerful will to see this through.

The day I finally told him about the memories I carried—the scars I'd carefully hidden under layers and layers of armor—he didn't flinch. No matter what I threw at him, he didn't run. I told him they might never heal—he said we'd work it through together. I told him that some days are worse than others—he said he'd be

there for them.

I said I didn't like to be touched.

He knew as well as I did that even talking about it was the same as letting him in to touch.

Turned out, I was looking at this all wrong from the start. As Remy says in *Gambit* 16, "Roguey, we spent so much time worryin' about your powers keepin' us from havin' a real relationship when all it took was a bit of . . . tweakin' on my powers instead!"

I just needed to find the right person willing to "tweak" their powers for mine.

If I ever manage to go back in time, like the X-Men, I'd tell the ten-year-old me how important it is to watch all the *X-Men* cartoons with her brother. I'd tell the teenage me to be sure to get that job at the comic store, and don't worry about the convenient lie about buying the special anniversary edition issue for that brother—just get it, and enjoy.

I wouldn't need to tell the eighteen-year-old me, with the picture of Gambit and Rogue on that mix CD, anything—she got it.

And I know that if I did manage to go back in time, the younger me would laugh and swear that everything was *fine*. That I didn't need stuff like comics and superheroes and *love*. That of course everything would be all right, because the young me didn't know about things like depression and rage and cutting herself up to bleed the demons out.

But Rogue and Gambit knew. I watched them work it out, all the while utterly oblivious to my own feelings, unaware how much I envied Rogue her Remy. Even now, there are times when I think about the pieces that came together—the TV show, the job, the comic I stumbled into—and I shake my head. I know without a shred of doubt that had he not given me that CD, with *that* cover, I wouldn't have let down my guard enough to give him the chance I did. Because I didn't think he'd understand.

And I would have been so wrong.

I never did tell him how much I loved Rogue and Gambit, even after he'd given me his heart on a CD cover. These days, he doesn't have to ask. Somehow, he knows. And on the days when the demons that still live inside my psyche get too much, or the anxieties and self-doubt start itching and I flash back to that little girl sobbing in a stranger's house, the man I married puts his arms around me and drawls, "Don' you worry 'bout it none, *chère*."

Because that's what superheroes do. They save lives.

SPIDER-MANHATTAN

SCOTT WESTERFELD

When I first visited Manhattan at the age of twelve, I looked up and said, "So *this* is where Spider-Man can fly."

I was raised in Palo Alto, suburban Houston, and small-town Connecticut—all places without skyscrapers. The odd billboard or water tower jutted into the sky, but there was never a succession of heights to swing from. In these flatlands, Spider-Man could run fast and shoot goo from his wrists, but that was about it. And a ground crawler is hardly Spider-Man at all.

Before that visit, I'd assumed that the Manhattan of Marvel Comics was a made-up place. All those gargoyles to alight on, awnings to bounce from, and flagpoles for quick changes of direction seemed too convenient, too Spidey friendly. Like the steam rising from manhole covers in movies, I assumed that this urban terrain was a product of artistic license, a way to make the proportional abilities of a spider add up to something more super than they really were.

But in those first moments in Times Square, looking up, I discovered all those perches and projections to be real, waiting for anyone spidery enough to use them. It turned out that Spider-Man had been invented to match Manhattan, not the other way around. He was the embodiment of real urban geometries. (Bonus points: the streets were steaming, too!)

That was the beginning of my love of New York City. It's the place where Spider-Man can fly. Where we all can fly, a little.

New York is full of metonymies given form. Here you discover that Madison is a real avenue, Wall an actual street. But for twelve-year-old me, advertising and finance were boring, while swinging from building to building and fighting crime was *awesome*. This was a kind of flying that was within my reach. Back in Palo Alto, my older sisters and I had hung a rope from a tree and swung from our second-story window to the ground. (It was the olden days, when kids were allowed to do such things.) This was super-heroing at a human scale.

Superman always flew too high for me. He felt too remote, like when you look down from an aircraft, and the sights are reduced to the abstractions of radial irrigation and urban planning. No people, just squares and circles.

Of course, in the mid-seventies Superman was fighting Blackrock, Faora, and Atomic Skull, whose vast powers made them feel alien (if they weren't literally aliens in the first place). Spider-Man, on the other hand, still punched the odd mugger. His proximity to the ground, his sticky connections to the architecture around him, kept him attached to reality. He wasn't looking down from an airplane; he was looking down from a half-dozen stories up, where the buzz of the city still trembled.

It was always heroes like Spidey, patrolling at gargoyle level, who felt gritty and relevant to me. They perched, jumped, and swung, using the geometries of the buildings themselves to get around, a mode of travel that embraced the city in all its specificity.

Comic book scripts sometimes call this the "rooftop express," and these days it's a default trope of superhero travel. Everyone seems to have a grappling hook, a long horizontal leap, and a love of mixing expositional dialogue with metahuman parkour. But Spidey was the original rooftop bounder, the embodiment of skyline travel, and Manhattan was perfect for him.

Because it was *designed* to be that way.

Near the end of the nineteenth century, steel-frame architecture was invented, increasing the practical height of buildings tenfold. But as the first wave of skyscrapers began to arise in Chicago and New York, city planners worried that sheer walls of concrete would block out sunlight and air from the streets below. Would this create a cold, dark maze that would drive puny human city dwellers to madness?

The race for the sky kept going unregulated, until the forty-story Equitable Building was completed in 1915. This sheer-walled tower sat on a plot of only a single acre, but it cast a seven-acre shadow across its surroundings. Suddenly sunlight itself had become a resource in limited supply.

In answer, the NYC Council passed the 1916 Zoning Resolution, which codified setbacks for Manhattan skyscrapers. A new geometry was created in the urban jungle, a theoretical incline called the "sky exposure plane." This plane extends upward at an angle in both directions from every public street, defining a volume of space that must be kept empty. The practical effect of this ordnance was to force new buildings into the cake-tiered, art deco profile that became Manhattan's signature. This open area allowed sunlight down into the canyoned streets and created a stratum reserved for all those gargoyles, flagpoles, balconies, and other perches beloved of Spider-Man and his roof-crawling colleagues.

The familiar Spider-Manhattan of today was born.

I started climbing buildings in college. In high school I'd already done a bit of "urban spelunking," to use a somewhat garish term, exploring the crawl spaces of my high school. My friends and I discovered how to access the area above the auditorium, from which we spied on drama classes, and other hidden pathways. We also discovered the joys of fiberglass insulation, which created a subtle day-long itch in our clothes (and possibly damaged our lungs).

But it was at college that a mix of modern and Gothic architecture tempted me to climb the *outsides* of buildings. Vassar had terraces and roof ways aplenty, mostly at the six-story height, that median altitude for web crawling: low enough to be connected to the ground, yet high enough to survey with heroic omniscience.

The new Walker Field House, with its parabolic curves, was particularly compelling. It was under construction late in my junior year, with ropes still running down from its spires for hauling up building materials. I spent the night of my twentieth birthday swinging from them, sliding across the late-spring rime that coated the building.

But it wasn't until I moved to NYC after graduation that my love of rooftops came full circle and my affair with Spider-Manhattan truly began.

In nineteenth-century New York, the ground floors were where rich people lived. Before elevators, life above the third floor was onerous, and above the sixth, unthinkable. Attics had always been reserved for servants and stepchildren, after all.

This all changed in 1925, with Emery Roth's Ritz Tower and Condé Nast's duplex apartment, both situated on Park Avenue. Instead of laundry rooms and servants' quarters, the upper floors of the Ritz had terraced garden apartments with city-spanning views. And though Nast's penthouse was a Frankenstein's monster cobbled together from what were maid's rooms on the building plans, by the end of the Roaring Twenties his rooftop parties were the most fashionable in the city. In very short order, class and privilege had switched positions with servitude on the vertical scale of Manhattan.

Of course, not every building in NYC has an elevator,

so this reversal of rich and poor did not universally apply. And once again, zoning laws made their presence felt. In 1929, walk-ups were limited by law to six stories (or sixty feet). Soon two distinct Manhattans took shape: the lofty, elevator-equipped spires of the fancy precincts, with their setbacks and gargoyles, and the walk-up tenement neighborhoods with their ragged five- and six-story skylines.

The latter is, of course, where most people fresh out of college live, and where I found myself seeking out top-floor apartments to rent, that perfect altitude for the rooftop express. Like a superhero on patrol, I felt most connected at six stories or so, where snatches of conversation drifted up, and the little dramas unfolding below could be witnessed and understood. Where people weren't ants, but people. My apartment was still high enough to be a refuge, to keep me above the fray. And on the roof with a beer, I found myself almost at the level of flight.

Not boring, too-high Superman flight, of course. Spider-Manhattan flight—that stickier, more complicated traversal of the details and geometries of the city, as messy as Peter Parker's finances or his personal life.

I don't climb buildings anymore, but five years ago, while writing a book about airships, I took a research ride in an actual Zeppelin. The craft stayed close enough to the ground that dogs barked at us, and we could *see* them barking. We could peek into backyards and alleys from above. It was more intimate than any airplane, always closer to the ground than the tallest skyscrapers.

I've lived in eight apartments since college, across many kinds of neighborhoods. Some new places I moved to; some shifted into place around me. I've lived in dangerous, gentrified, petit bourgeois, and downright fancy areas, and in various transitional or layered combinations thereof. What I've learned is that I'm happy in any of these, as long as I'm between the fifth and eighth floor. It turns out that what I care about is not my neighborhood's attitudes, but my own *altitude*. Where I want to live is at that border between an elevator and a walk-up, between outright flight and parkour, between rooftop and sky.

Even when I'm down on the street, in the thick of things, I'm looking up into the terrain of that sky exposure plane—into the eyes of those gargoyles, along the nooks and crannies of the rooftop express, those juts and recesses that give Manhattan its character and history, and give Spider-Man a place to fly.

HOW I SPENT MY SUMMER VACATION WITH THE JUDAS CONTRACT

BRAD MELTZER

I was fourteen. She was sixteen.

I had a long, shaggy bowl cut (feathered on the sides, natch). She had a blond Dutch-boy hairstyle.

I was at the height of puberty. She was far more experienced.

I was an innocent. She was, too (or so it seemed).

Her name was Terra (aka Tara Markov). And she was the first girl to break my heart.

Simply put, she lied to me. And I'm not just talking about the standard grade school lies ("You're *definitely* my best friend," or "I never told Julie Lerner you were fat."). I'm talking something far more sinister. Terra betrayed me. She deceived me. She shoved a knife in my belly and sliced upward all the way to my heart. And at fourteen years old, I loved every minute of it.

To back up a bit, and to give a little background in the hope that, when my mother reads this, she won't feel the parental guilt that will cause her to spend the next year of my life asking, "Who's this Tara Markov, and how come you didn't tell me about her?" here's a quick primer. In December 1982, *New Teen Titans* 26 was published, introducing Terra, a troubled fifteen-year-old who became the first new member of the Teen Titans. Let me make one thing clear: this was a big deal to me.

In 1982, *New Teen Titans,* written by Marv Wolfman and drawn oh so exquisitely by George Pérez, was easily the best book on the market (that's right, I said it—and, yes, smart guy, I'm well aware that Byrne-Claremont *X-Men* was being published at the same time). Made up of the "junior" superheroes of the DC Universe, the Titans brought together such mainstays as Robin, Kid Flash, and Wonder Girl, with new characters Cyborg, Starfire, Raven, and Changeling, a (young, green—yes, green) fifteen-year-old class clown who could change into green animals (yes, green, and, yes, animals). As I type those words, I'm reminded that comics always suffer in the retelling, but take my word for it, the alchemy between Wolfman and Pérez created a vehicle for stories that redefined what comic book characterization was all about. Sure, the Titans beat on the bad guys, but the book was first and foremost about the relationships between these young kids who were saddled with enough power to knock down a mountain. And you thought your puberty was tough.

Which brings us back to Terra. At the time she was invited to join, the Titans were a family. Seven members. And now there was an eighth. As I said, it was a big deal—imagine Ringo telling the other Beatles, "Hey, blokes—I got a great fifth to play tambourine!" Still, it was accepted without much fuss. Let's not forget, that's how superteams work. Members leave . . . members join. Even Batman and Robin parted ways (the original Robin, fanboy). There are no Beatles in comics.

As Terra spent time with the group, there were definitely a few doubters. Would she fit in? Was she joining the team with the right intentions? But me? I was like Changeling—simply smitten.

I'm not ashamed. I was twelve when she first appeared. Wonder Woman was far too old, and Wonder Girl was mature enough that she was dating a guy with a beard. Dammit, where were the teenage girls who'd like insecure, loudmouthed boys wearing Lee jeans like me? And then, out of the George Pérez blue sky, comes this fifteen-year-old fast-talking blonde with superpowers who could control the Earth itself. You better believe the ground quaked beneath my feet. Sure, she was trying to blow up the Statue of Liberty, but that was only because terrorists were threatening to kill her parents if she didn't take Lady Liberty down. She didn't want to do it, though—remember her words? "I don't want to do any of this!" Look at the back issues. There were tears in her eyes as she begged Changeling to stay away. "Don't make it harder on me," she begged. "Please!!" No question, this was a girl who needed help. She needed someone to come to her aid. She needed me.

Fast-forward to issue 28: Terra was robbing a bank.

Like before, her heart wasn't in it. She even apologized to Changeling as she attacked him. "I'm really sorry I have to do this—" And again, there were the tears. Curse those tears! They melted my pubescent heart like Fire Lad tonguing a Klondike bar. Dammit, world, can't you understand she's only doing it to save her parents!?

Of course, the Titans understood, and helped her track down the terrorists, only to find that her parents were already dead(!). Raging out of control, Terra screamed for revenge, gripping the terrorists in an enormous fist made of rock. As the villains begged for mercy, my girl squeezed them tighter. The Earth was shaking. She was so powerful, she started an earthquake. My young eyes went wide as the stone fist tightened— I couldn't believe it—she was really gonna kill 'em. But like all true heroes, as Terra peered into the abyss, she didn't like what she saw. Crumbling to her knees, she showed the villains the mercy never given to her parents. Again, my heart plummeted—Terra was fifteen and all alone in the world. Didn't anyone hear what she was saying on the final pages? "I . . . feel so alone." And then, Changeling looked into those sad, newly orphaned blue eyes and said exactly what my twelve-year-old brain was thinking: "You don't have to be, Terra. *I'm* here." (Emphasis not mine, but man, it could've been.) The teaser on the cover of the issue said INTRODUCING TERRA! IS SHE FRIEND—OR FOE? "Friend!" I shouted. "Friend!"

I have to hand it to Wolfman and Pérez. They knew what they were doing. Preying on the knight-in-shining-

armor gene that's inherent in every male comic fan (oh,
c'mon, why do you think we read this stuff in the first place?), they conjured the perfect young lady in distress, then stepped back to watch us put our legs in the metal trap. The first step was done. By introducing her as a victim, they made us feel for her. But then they raised the stakes. Sure, she was in pain, but she was far from helpless. In fact, when Changeling tried to come to her aid, she not only refused it, she actually punched him in the face, called him a nerd, and flew away. Think about that a moment. Do you have any idea what a strong female character like that does to a thirteen-year-old psyche? No? Then let me back up even further and explain.

In 1981, in the heart of New York–accent Brooklyn, my biggest social dilemma was deciding between Karen Akin and Ananda Bresloff. The slam books (aka, *popularity ratings* that were passed around to decide our social fates) were clear: given the choices "good," "fair," and "yuk," both Karen and Ananda had ranked me as "good." Even in fifth grade, "good" was a good sign. Now the ball was in my court. How would I rank them? Sure, we had traded slam books at the exact same time, but only a fool ranks someone before they see how that person ranks them. Make no mistake, I may've been dumb enough to think my knee-high tube socks were cool, and even insecure enough to want to wear a gold Italian-horn charm around my neck even though I was Jewish, but I was nobody's fool. And so, I handed Karen and Ananda their respective slam books.

"Did you do the chart?" they asked.

"Of course," I said.

But when they checked inside, here's what they saw:

GIRLS	GOOD	FAIR	YUK*
Darlene Signorelli		X	
Randi Boxer		X	
Danielle Levy		X	
Ananda Bresloff			
Karen Akin			

That's right, bubba. I left it blank. Who'd they think they were dealing with? I read far too many Lex Luthor stories—every single Adventure Comics digest and the oversized maxibooks—to fall for some simple trap. I wasn't putting my heart on the line until I knew it was a sure thing. And so, armed with my recent "good" ranking, I knew who I was deciding between. Time to make a choice.

Here's how it looked to me in fifth grade: Ananda was really cute, nice, soft-spoken, and really cute. Karen was loud; had a face full of freckles; and, thanks to her older sister, seemed to have far more experience than everyone else in the class combined. She knew how to write in cursive before anyone—and told us all what a blow job was. She was tough, too. More important, she made fun

---

* Author's note: Every one of these girls was outrageously cute. But in fifth grade, only a schmuck would throw a "Good" to everyone. A few years back, I heard Danielle became a model. Who's the schmuck now?

of me and pushed me around. Even back then, the choice was clear. Now I just had to break the news.

It was the last day of school in fifth grade at P.S. 206. I'd spent weeks going through slam books and leaving Karen and Ananda's rankings blank. But today was the day that would all change. In fact, if I summoned the strength in time, I might even be picking my first girlfriend. The clock was ticking toward three. The school year was almost gone. Forever melodramatic, I waited until the final bell rang. I remember putting my little checkmarks in the appropriate columns, then slamming the book shut before anyone got a peek. As we all ran for the doors, flooding into the school yard, I handed the book back to its owner. I still remember her flipping through the pages to see my answer. She looked up when she saw it: Karen—good; Ananda—yuk.* Yet before anyone could even react, I—being the brave young soul that I was—darted from the school yard and ran straight home without talking to anyone. The next morning, I left for camp. Two months went by before I'd have to face my decision. Was I a wuss or a genius? All I knew was, when I returned to Brooklyn in early September, Karen was my girlfriend, even if she did push me around and completely intimidate me.

So what's this have to do with Terra? Simply put, I was a Karen guy, not an Ananda guy. Maybe it was young masochism, maybe it was just a love of being dominated—but when it came to choosing sides, back then, I wanted

---

* Ananda was so cute. No doubt about it. I today blame my choice on my need to see things in black and white.

the tough chick. Karen was tough—which is why we broke up soon after. Then, in June 1983, my dad lost his job and my family moved from Brooklyn to Miami, Florida. When we first arrived, I didn't have a single friend, much less a girlfriend. No Karen . . . no Ananda . . . nothing. It was right around the time Terra joined the Titans. At first glance, she was tough, too. And she had superpowers. She mouthed off at Changeling and definitely pushed him around. No doubt, she could kick Karen Akin's ass. Truthfully, she could kick my ass. And with that soft spot she had from her parents' recent death . . . it didn't take three issues for Wolfman and Pérez to achieve their goal . . . I was now a Terra guy.

Laugh if you must, but it was a great infatuation. My father's generation loved Lois Lane, who always needed her Superman. I loved Terra, who didn't need me, didn't want me, and could pummel me with fifty tons of rock if I really pissed her off. Forget Black Canary in her fishnets. Here was someone my age, wounded by the loss of lost parents and searching for a soul mate. It was a potent combination for us young comic readers. Before Madonna made strong women cool and Gwen Stefani made them hot, Terra was the first official grrl for the new generation. True love indeed.

For the next six months of my life, I watched as the kind, happy family of the Teen Titans welcomed this hardened orphan into their midst. She helped them fight the Brotherhood of Evil, Thunder and Lightning, and even the Titans' most feared enemy, Deathstroke.

Whatever concerns they had about her were quickly silenced. Month after month, Terra put her life on the line for the team. Within six issues (a lifetime in comics, or a day, depending on the story line), she was one of the Titans' own, enmeshed in their personal lives just as much as she was enmeshed in my own. Then came the final pages of *New Teen Titans* 34.

I'll never forget—it was a right-hand page, perfectly placed so the surprise wouldn't be revealed until us readers casually flipped past the DC house ads. I turned the page and there it was: in a rundown tenement, Terra was secretly meeting with *Deathstroke!* Her face was lit with a dark grin I'd never seen on her. *My God, they were working together!* My eyes stayed locked on her mask, which she twirled carelessly around a come-hither pointer finger. My world was spinning just as fast. It was like Batgirl sleeping with the Joker! She was plotting the Titans' downfall with their greatest enemy. I trusted her! I was there for her! And unlike any other comic creation I'd ever read, and I say this in the least creepy way possible, *I loved her!* And now, she was reaching down my throat and ripping my heart out for her own enjoyment! *Terra, how could you betray me like this!?*

And now, a word from reality . . . Okay, so it wasn't that bad—but I also don't want to undersell the moment. I can still remember my stomach sinking down to my testicles. In the world of comics, nothing like this had ever happened. Sure, there were always heroes who were later revealed as villains. At Marvel, the Avengers did it every week: "There Shall Be . . . *a Traitor Among Us!*" Both Black Panther and Wonder Man were originally there to infiltrate the Avengers . . . the Falcon was created by the Red Skull to kill Captain America . . . even Snapper Carr took a potshot at the Justice League. But the end of those stories was always the same: the so-called villain (Black Panther, Wonder Man, Falcon, Snapper) came to their senses and saved the day. In Terra's case, however . . . this girl didn't just infiltrate the Titans—she really wanted to kill them. And best of all, as the months wore on, Wolfman and Pérez never backed away from the decision. Indeed, issue after issue, they kept turning up the despicable meter on Terra's actions. By the time they were done, Terra wasn't just working with Deathstroke, she was sleeping with him. Let's see Black Panther do that.

For my now-thirteen-year-old brain, it was all too much. Don't get me wrong, I wasn't turned off by what she was doing. C'mon, I was thirteen. She was the first true femme fatale in my life. I was turned *on*. I can still remember the slutty eye shadow they put on her when she was in villain mode, smoking a cigarette like a young blond Britney Spears doing Marlene Dietrich doing bad eighties porn. There were even high-heeled pumps scattered across the floor by the (wait for it) beanbag chair. So scary . . . but somehow . . . *so naughty*. Which brings me back to my old girlfriend, Karen Akin.

In August 1984, I'd been living in Florida for over a year. I was now the new kid who sat silently in the middle row of the class. No one knew my name. Sure, I'd made a few friends, but it was nothing like Karen, Ananda, or any of the other girls from Brooklyn. All I had was Terra. The only question was: How was it all gonna end?

The final chapter of "The Judas Contract" was published in *Tales of the Teen Titans Annual* 3 during that same summer of 1984. It was titled "Finale." By then, all the cards were on the Titans Tower table: Terra was working (and sleeping) with Deathstroke, all the Titans (except Dick Grayson) were defeated and captured, and Nightwing and Jericho were in the midst of a near-impossible rescue attempt in the heart of H.I.V.E. headquarters. No doubt, it all came down to this: Terra would either remain the villain or come to her senses and save the day. I still remember looking at the cover, trying to guess the answer. Pérez made the choice clear: on one side were all the Titans, on the other was Deathstroke and the H.I.V.E. Terra was in the middle, her head turned back slightly toward Changeling, who seemed to be pleading for her redemption. To play with our heads even more, Pérez added two worry lines by Terra's face, as if she, too, were struggling with the decision. I made my guess. There was no way Terra was truly evil. Redemption was a few pages away.

Forty pages later, Terra was dead. I shook my head as the scene played out. Changeling begged her to come to her senses . . . he pleaded and prayed . . . but Terra's rage was all consuming. Remembering the cover, I kept waiting for her to look back at him and see true love. Or hope. Or the family who loved her. But it never came. Eyes wide with insanity, she attacked with a ruthlessness I'd never seen in a comic—and in the end, as a mountain of self-propelled rocks rained down and buried her, that rage—literally and figuratively—killed her. I shook my head. *There's no way she's dead,* I told myself. I don't care what the omniscient narrator said. I know my comics. Hero or villain, Terra was too good a character. Until they find a body—

"We found Tara's body," Wonder Girl said one page later. I turned to another right-hand page and there was Changeling . . . down on his knees, clutching Terra's broken corpse as her arms sagged lifelessly toward the ground. Self-destruction complete.

I still can't believe they went through with it. A few years ago, I read an interview with George Pérez that said Terra was created to die, and they never planned on taking the easy way out by suddenly writing the happy ending. I hope they know how much that decision affected me as a writer. Old girlfriends and teenage fetishes aside, it was one of the most heartbreaking stories I'd ever read. They took people in capes and utility belts and made them real—and just when we loved them most . . . just when we opened our arms to embrace them . . . Wolfman and Pérez stabbed ice picks in our armpits and did the one thing neither Marvel nor DC ever had the balls to do—they kept her as a villain and slaughtered her. She was sixteen. No redemption. No feel-good music during the end credits. The pulp side of the genre has it right—it's always best when the femme fatale buys it in the end—but in comics, it'd never been done. And the traitor side of the story? Wonder Man, Falcon, Black Panther, and even Snapper got honorary memberships. Terra got a headstone with her name on it.

To this day, "The Judas Contract" is one of the few stories that actually surprised me—not just in its ending but in how it plucked at my emotions. As I said, Terra lied to me, betrayed me, and stomped on my trust with her six-inch heels. Without a doubt, I loved every second of it.

SUPERHEROES AND WRITING

HOW BATMAN
SAVED MY LIFE

JOE R. LANSDALE

Forgive me. Like Kurt Vonnegut's character Billy Pilgrim, in the course of this essay I will come unstuck in time.

The world was gray.

Sometimes there were darker and lighter shades, but those were rare. For me the world was mostly a gummy gray, and maybe a little sad. I don't know why exactly, but my earliest memories are of hot, boring days and a strange feeling of the ground being close to my feet, the sky too close to my head. When I moved, it was as if that gummy grayness was thick and sticky, a kind of soul-sucking molasses that restricted my movements and clogged my thinking. I felt this way, and I was only a child.

I lived in a small town where everyone had small-town dreams. I'm not criticizing a small-town dream. A high school education, a solid job with a hope of retirement, that's a dream a lot of people had when they came back from World War II and still have. I have certainly done my share of hard-core work, farming, factory, etc., and I have wished for security and a calm retirement without having to live under a bridge, licking the secret sauce off discarded McDonald's hamburger wrappers. I understand the appeal, but not enough to look at it as a lifelong ambition.

In the fifties and early sixties I was a child growing up in a fresh world that after the war wanted peace and certainty. People wanted a "normal" life. They wanted stability. They wanted their children to have the same sort of stability but a better run at it, more money and a larger view of the world. College, a steady well-paying job, and then a nice company pension to go with what was then called an old age pension, and is now called social security. For them, that was having your chocolate cake with fine, white icing and eating it, too.

My parents were different. My father could neither read nor write, but he had his own small ambitions, and the main one was to be a self-employed mechanic. Eventually he managed just that. He and my mom worked for themselves mostly, though they both had standard jobs from time to time, and their desire for independence may have had something to do with my childhood restlessness.

Early on I learned that I was unlike other kids in my thinking and my interests. What interested them bored me, and what interested me confused many of them. I was always reaching for something I couldn't grasp or even recognize.

And then my sister-in-law, Mary, who was married to

my brother John, who was seventeen years older than me, brought me a stack of comic books. I was probably three or four at the time. They were funny animal comics, things of that nature. When I opened them, the world shifted slightly on its axis and it was flooded with electric-spark colors and a cacophony of internal sounds and emotions. The gummy world loosened up. The sky went high and the ground became solid and not so close.

Mary read those comics to me, and soon, much to her chagrin, because I couldn't get enough, I kept bringing them to her to have her read them to me over and over again. She read them so much, I memorized them, and then, before long I was reading them for myself. Ravenous for words, I was like a man constantly hungry with a large spoon and the best food in the world on a table before him. Bottom line is I learned to read from comics, and everything I became as an adult came from them.

My first love was Superman, and what child wouldn't want to have superpowers and a secret sliding-door closet with robots that looked just like you? You could send one to school to represent you, while the real you rescued people, blew out fires with superbreath, burned holes in walls with heat vision to get at criminals, or just used X-ray vision to look through walls to see what was going on. I was too young then to think of what teenage boys would think of when they thought about X-ray vision, but I damn well knew it was cool. And there was flying, superstrength, invulnerability, immortality, traveling into the depths of space without need of a breathing apparatus or even a spaceship, and there was the ability to travel through time, if I just flew fast enough, and so on and so on.

Pretty soon, though, I realized I wasn't going to be Superboy or Superman, and another character caught my imagination like a butterfly in a net. He seemed more of a possibility.

Batman.

The Batman comics I was reading were the Silver Age Batman comics, and he was somewhat different from the original creation and most certainly different from the Batman of today. But he was, as Batman has always been, an ordinary man who put his body and mind to use, became strong and well trained in acrobatics and martial arts and criminal science. He was Doc Savage and Sherlock Holmes and the Shadow all rolled into one. He was at that time, however, considerably more of a milquetoast than now. He was a representative of the status quo in many ways, but we kids always knew that underneath that sheen of shiny conservatism there was something dark and exciting, teasing the edge of the line, while at the same time remaining fair and honest and admirable. The Batman of the fifties and early sixties may have seemed a wise father figure with a sidekick and son substitute named Robin; but, as I said, when we readers thought about the Bat Cave and Batman's fluttering cloak in the dark of the night, we knew there was more to him than flag waving and eat your vegetables and don't leave oily rags in a closet where they might catch fire. He was more than the day-to-day life I saw being lived around me. I was too young, perhaps, to see the beauty in that day-to-day life, the satisfying order it held for some. For me, I needed a bit of chaos in my existence. Color explosions. Outlets for creative thinking. Some way to let the ordinary seep out of my head and the fantastic seep in. It's not that I thought my needs were superior to those of others, but I did know they were in fact my needs, and I wanted them met. Comics were the door.

That said, I was an ordinary man. I was not given superpowers by a yellow sun. I was not given superspeed by a lightning bolt and a chemical splash. I waited for an alien to recognize my bravery and integrity, come down, and give me a powerful ring that would respond to my will, but the alien did not come. The closest I got to being Aquaman was splashing water out of the tub and commanding a rubber duck to my bidding. It dawned on me that since Batman possessed no superpowers, that maybe I had a chance to be like him.

So you can understand why I immediately wanted to be Batman. I wanted to be smart and strong and save people. It would have been nice if I had the money Batman inherited as part of the Wayne family fortune, but I figured if I could get my mother to make me a cowl and cape, I would be on my way. Maybe I could come by the money later, though obviously not from inheritance.

She did make me a cape and cowl, bless her wonderful heart. She put cardboard in the ears to make them stand

HOW BATMAN SAVED MY LIFE

up, but they wavered at the base and flapped about like the ears of a chastised German shepherd. And my poor nephew, who was only a few years younger than me, became Robin. He had a costume, too. Same as in the comics. My mother was quite the seamstress.

We wore our costumes about the house and in the yard, and ran about and climbed trees and waited for crimes to happen, solved some invisible ones. I read everything I could on fingerprints and solving crimes, battling criminals. I even had a chemistry set, as Batman had, only I found the best I could do was make water turn blue or violet. I don't remember what I added to do that, or why this was important, but that was about the extent of my knowledge, though I did blow a test tube up once by mixing materials that it said not to mix. Unlike Batman, chemistry and math were not my forte.

Years later, my enthusiasm for Batman would lead to me studying martial arts, something I've done now for fifty-one years and something that led to me creating an accredited martial arts system of my own, Shen Chuan. It also led to great curiosity, as Batman exhibited, and that led to a desire to know a lot about everything; and there is nothing more beneficial and necessary to becoming a writer than curiosity. It trumps all else, actually.

Unlike Batman, I didn't manage to be much of an acrobat, and I didn't have the ability to learn about everything, as I had hoped, and I didn't have the money for a cool Batmobile or Batplane. What I did have was that cowl and cape and a somewhat unwilling sidekick who would

probably have preferred the Batman outfit and me dressed
as Robin. I remember thinking we should come up with
some kind of Bat-Signal that we could give the police
commissioner to use when he needed us, but our little
berg of Mount Enterprise only had about 150 people living in town at the time and no police commissioner, so
that didn't seem likely. As for getting to those crimes,
we had bicycles—no car or plane—and a submarine
seemed impractical in the nearby but shallow creek.

Still, we prepared. We practiced running and swinging our fists at imaginary villains, kicking and throwing
each other around—sometimes we had to be our own
villains. We had utility belts, too, though they were short
on supplies. Rubber bands, paper clips, some notes with
information written on them about fingerprints or some
such, some empty pockets for collecting crime samples,
if in fact that actually came up. As best as possible, we
were ready.

Then the local bank got robbed. We found out about it
the morning after a good night's sleep. So much for crime
fighting. That sort of took the wind out of my sails. If
there wasn't a Bat-Signal to let me know when I was
needed, how was I to help? And what if the signal came
on and I was sleeping? It didn't work like a siren. I had to
see it. Maybe a siren was the ticket, but again, there was
that whole no-police-commissioner problem. There
was also school to attend.

I began to see flaws in my career choice.

Gradually, the desire to be Batman faded, but not the

desire to be like him, at least in the ways that were possible for me. I continued to read Batman comics as I aged, and Batman matured, too, after going through an ultrasilly time in the 1960s, due to the insane popularity of the goofy TV show. Though, to be honest, the show pretty much was Batman as the comics presented him during the time I began reading him. It took the TV show for me to realize just how childish and silly a lot of it was back then, and how alike it was to the TV show with its Bat labels everywhere, the cornball dialogue, and moralizing. Hell, I had become older and wiser. I was almost a teenager.

There was Bat Change on the horizon, however, a newer, more modern, more realistic Batman, spurred onward by a transition in comics in general, a change brought about by Marvel. Their take on superheroes ran through the comic book world like a brush fire. Their heroes lived in the real world and they had real-world problems. They made comics better, and gradually Batman changed with them. But I never quite got over the Batman I first discovered, his obvious and intentionally honest and heroic nature. The new and greater depth of the character made him more interesting, but it was still that guy who wanted to do things right, wanted to give the underdog a chance, wanted to protect the weak that held my interest, and still does. I believed in fighting for the underdog. I believed in trying to keep your word and do the right thing. I believed that being a decent human being mattered; and that no matter how flawed I might be, there was always a guidepost I could measure myself by. The Batman of my youth.

I loved comics so much I wanted to write them and draw them. I actually made my own comics using colored pencils, folded paper stapled at the corners, stories complete with panels and word balloons. A lack of talent in the art department prevented my drawing them successfully, and I abandoned the idea of doing it all myself. I seemed to have some talent in the writing part of that equation, however, and I pursued it with the hopes that someday I might write for a comic book company. The love of comics led to my reading fiction, and lots of it, and pretty soon I knew I was going to be a writer. I thought about being other things as well, but nothing ever held me or called to me like writing, even if writing comic books alone had sort of drifted to the back of my ambitions. However, the desire to play with words and stories and to think in explosive colors had been stuck into my skull by comics, and it grew like a balloon being pumped rapidly with helium. Someday I knew there would be enough in it for it to take flight.

Unstuck in time again.

It took a few years, but my old dreams were taking shape. Not only had I made a career as a writer I was now being asked to write comics, and write for animated television programs about none other than Batman, and in one case, Superman, as well as Jonah Hex. I was so excited I could have eaten a box full of kitties—only evil kitties, of course.

Like Edgar Rice Burroughs, who I discovered some years after Batman, Bob Kane's creation gave my life color; it unstuck the gummy gray and tossed high the sky. Gave me all manner of hopes and dreams.

That burning desire, that brightness of color and cacophony of internal sounds and events have not ceased. Fact is, the colors of late have brightened even more, and that helium balloon I mentioned earlier has floated me high up, but not as high as I think I can go.

Each morning when I wake up and my feet hit the floor, I feel like the luckiest person who was ever born. I love my work. I love my life, and I certainly adore my family. I owe a large part of that to comics, and specifically to Batman.

He gave me my career, and I think those comics and the martial arts they inspired me to study, gave me a joy that led to my confidence to pursue my dreams, to take life by the throat and squeeze all the juice out of it. It has led to some financial success, an opportunity to travel, meet interesting people, and do amazing things that seemed pretty impossible and far away when I was a child living in East Texas in the fifties and sixties.

It's amazing to think what my life might have been like had I not been given those comics by my sister-in-law. Would the world still be gray and gummy, the earth and sky too close to the eye?

I can't say. But I sure wouldn't want to go back through time and take that chance. It's all been too wonderful.

Thank you, Caped Crusader. You saved another life, one outside of the comics, mine, and you gave me the greatest gift a person can receive.

The joy of living a creative life.

ALL THE WORLD
IS WAITING FOR YOU

CARRIE VAUGHN

One day in preschool, I must have been four or five, I was out on the playground being Wonder Woman. I did this by sticking my arms straight out and running around, back and forth in tight circles, making growling airplane noises. Because I wasn't just Wonder Woman, I was Wonder Woman in her invisible jet. (Wonder Woman is the coolest superhero because she has her own jet. She's not just a superhero, she's a *pilot!*)

Another girl stopped me. She was bigger than I was, and she wasn't smiling. "*What* are you *doing*?" she demanded.

"I'm Wonder Woman," I said. "In her invisible jet."

"You're doing it wrong. Wonder Woman in her invisible jet wouldn't look like *that*, she'd look like *this*." The big frowning girl then did this little half squat thing and shuffled around for a few feet as if sitting in the cockpit of an invisible jet.

I understood her point. I understood the straightforward realism she was striving for. Nevertheless, I had no response for her. To me, the correct answer was so blazingly obvious. My way may not have been realistic. But it was so much more fun. (I wonder now if my nemesis grew up to be one of those people who prefers that children not read about Harry Potter because magic isn't real. Or rather, they *think* magic isn't real.)

So I stuck my arms back out and kept running around, *flying*.

Sometimes I feel like I've spent a big chunk of my life defending the things I love.

So, the first thing Wonder Woman taught me was to stand up for what I like, and not to listen when other people tell me that what I like is stupid. You might think this is a simple thing, that it's the battle that all geeks learn to fight when they're teenagers and watching *Star Trek* when all their friends are into New Kids on the Block. (Wait, was that just me?) But this turned out to be very important later on.

Somewhere along the line, I'm not sure where or how, I became a great fan of literature. I know exactly when I became a writer (eighth grade English, best creative writing assignment ever, and I was the only one in class who was excited about it. Aha, maybe I'm onto something, I thought.), but the moment I became a passionate reader is a little fuzzy. Was it when I read *Charlotte's Web* when I was eight and cried and cried at the end, and wondered how a mere book could evoke such emotion?

Was it my freshman year of high school when I was enraged that the teacher had us reading an abridged version of *A Tale of Two Cities*? I read the complete version out of spite and found it so amazing, rich, emotional, and wonderful, I hated that teacher so much for passing off a pale, truncated version of that experience. As a senior in high school I read *Rosencrantz & Guildenstern Are Dead* side by side with *Hamlet*, and that might have shown me just what was possible with literature—not just literature but literature in conversation with itself. Literature is all about voices speaking to one another across centuries. I read *The Bell Jar* and felt like Sylvia Plath was talking just to me.

So I went to college and majored in English, and discovered something: not everyone liked the stories I liked. For many of my professors, science fiction and fantasy, anything that smacked of the unreal, was entirely verboten. Me? I'd never made a distinction. It was all literature.

My only creative writing class in college, the professor announced on the first day that she didn't want to see any science fiction or fantasy. I got the feeling this was an old battle for her—hence having to announce it right at the start, as if she anticipated having to read a bunch of postapocalyptic thrillers or wizarding adventures, heaven forbid any of us write about *superheroes*— and she needed to just nip that in the bud. Which really ought to have told her something about what her students *wanted* to write, but never mind that. According to her, there was "real" literature, and there was every-thing else. That's what she told me when I asked why no science fiction: "There's nothing you can do in science fiction that you can't do in real literature."

I went quiet. I wrote literary realism to make her happy. I was pretty good at it—but it wasn't very much fun. Much like shuffling along in a seated position while claiming to be Wonder Woman in her invisible jet. (Some people will tell you that literature—that writing—is not supposed to be fun. It's supposed to serious, peeling back layers of psyche to expose deep truths about the human condition. But you know what? You can do that and still have fun. I decided a while back that I was going to be a writer one way or another, and I could be serious about it, or I could have fun. Guess which I picked?)

If I had been smarter, wittier, more confident—not nineteen and confronting an actual writer and author-ity figure—I would have replied with algebra: If A equals B, and B equals C, then A equals C. If science fic-tion is doing the same thing as "real" literature—then it *is* real literature. To say otherwise is to be hung up on trappings.

I remembered Wonder Woman, and I started fighting battles. I wrote essays about fairy tales and their modern counterparts. I insisted on comparing Le Guin's *The Far-thest Shore* to Shakespeare's *The Tempest*—Ged and Prospero are both wizards at the end of their lives abdi-cating their powers and handing off the world to a

younger generation. They are the same story—a rite of
passage from authority into retirement. How can one be
literature and one not be?

I don't know that I actually ever pictured myself in
star-spangled shorts and a gold tiara, wielding a lasso to
force my professors to admit that, yes, they did in fact
read Tolkien and Le Guin and watch *Batman* when they
thought no one was looking. (We have an adorable picture of me when I was five years old in a homemade
Wonder Woman Halloween costume, with felt stars
pinned to blue shorts I already had.) But see, I didn't *care*
if they liked science fiction or not. I just wanted them to
stop telling other people not to like it and that they
couldn't read it.

That seemed very much like the kind of fight Wonder
Woman would get behind.

The second thing Wonder Woman taught me is that of
course women can be fighters and heroes. Of course
they can. What a stupid question. Why would we even
doubt such a thing?

And then I started reading the history of the genre and
the history of comic books, and I started writing and
publishing, and I realized that for some people this is
still an issue, and I think, *hoo boy*, we've got some work
to do. And then I imagine Lynda Carter's Wonder
Woman brushing off her hands after she's just beaten up

a roomful of bad guys and I feel much better. That's me, every single time I finish writing a story. Straightening my shoulders and throwing the universe a big smile.

I've argued that the whole generation of us authors who made up the wave of post-*Buffy* urban fantasy—all those novels about kick-ass women battling unknown creatures of the night—were able to write our heroines because we grew up with Lynda Carter's Wonder Woman. We took for granted that a woman could fight while wearing awesome clothes and smiling charmingly. Or shaking her head wryly at Steve's latest bungle. I've sat on an endless number of panels with titles along the lines of "What Is Up with All These Kick-ass Women Characters?" or "Strong Women Characters: Where the Hell Did They All Come from All of a Sudden?" (I may be paraphrasing here.) And I always say: Lynda Carter. I mean, we also had Lindsay Wagner's Bionic Woman, Sigourney Weaver's Ripley, Linda Hamilton's Sarah Connor, and so on. But Lynda Carter's Wonder Woman was the first, and because of her a whole generation of women writers completely accepted that a woman can be physically present and active in an adventure story. And that she can also be kind, funny, determined, angry, and everything, really.

It's hard to state the importance of this character, especially that particular incarnation of her. Not just for me but for my whole generation. She came out of the energy of second wave feminism in the 1970s. But my generation, and the next generation—the ones who are fighting for good representation of women in film, TV, and video games, the ones who are calling out harassment at conventions, the ones who are keeping feminism alive and gaining ground—one of the reasons we keep fighting is because of her. Because we remember, and because we took for granted that we would always have her. We see now that isn't true. We can lose that awesome strong Wonder Woman if we aren't careful. We have to keep her alive.

I have so much gratitude for Wonder Woman—and Lynda Carter—because she fought a really big fight that I didn't have to go on and fight. I can write about women lead characters in action adventure stories because she was there as a role model. If I'd had to try to break that ground—well, it's hard to imagine, and I'm very glad I didn't have to do that. But I'll damn well fight to keep these characters around.

The third thing Wonder Woman taught me: we must pass down these lessons to the next generation. We have Paradise Island, but it exists in our hearts and minds, and only if we keep talking about it. And the battles are never over. We have to protect our island of awesome women characters.

Three years ago, I became an aunt. My niece has my blond hair, and my brother, her father, is determined to raise her in a geek household. It's my job as the Bohemian aunt to make Halloween costumes, which I'm happy to do. This past Halloween, my niece asked to be Wonder Woman. I'm assured that she asked this on her own, unprompted. I spent a brief second wondering where she learned about Wonder Woman, what her first encounter with the icon was. I so clearly remember how I learned about her, after all. But it seems that Wonder Woman is just part of Emmy's world, like blue skies and Halloween. How cool is that? I'm a little envious.

I made a skirt that she can spin in, with sparkly holographic stars, to go with her WW logo T-shirt, a golden sash and wrist bands, and a tiara. On Halloween, she wore her pink cowboy boots with the costume, which was a perfect choice, I think. I for one am not going to tell her how she can or can't be Wonder Woman. That's for each fan to decide for herself.

THE DEVIL INSIDE

HOW MATT WAGNER'S GRENDEL SAVED MY LIFE

BRENDAN DENEEN

What am I doing on this roof wearing a superhero costume? I thought, staring out through my mask into the inky darkness of my small Connecticut town, tensing for action.

Wait . . . I'm getting ahead of myself. I need to pull back a little bit. Let's try that again.

The devil gets into all of us.

Yes, that's better.

Sometimes it's a small devil, sometimes it's a big one. And it can happen when you least expect it, and usually when you're the most vulnerable. For me, that was way back in 1988 when I was a sophomore in high school, long before Facebook or e-mail or cell phones (even before cable TV for me, since my family never had it).

I've always been told that "sophomore" is Latin for "Wise Fool." Psh, I was more like an Insane Idiot. An Uncontrollable Maniac. A Disheveled Rabble Rouser. You get the idea.

I was fifteen, finally starting to come into my own after years of being smaller than everyone else and kind of stuck in the middle. Or more accurately, the bottom—my oldest brother was known for being both insanely smart and a talented musician; my next oldest brother was known for being both handsome (his nickname in high school was literally "Rambo") and extremely athletic. As for me, I wasn't terribly smart, or athletic, or cool, or popular. I was one of maybe five kids in my school who read comic books (or at least one of five who admitted to it), which certainly didn't help matters. Sure, I had landed on the varsity tennis team freshman year but that wasn't exactly a badge of social honor, and neither was the fact that I starred in most of the school plays. I wasn't a full-blown nerd, even though I knew more about comic books than almost anyone in my town, and I wasn't exactly a jock, which was especially tough because my dad was a well-known basketball and baseball coach in town, and "Rambo" had been a high school basketball star.

And if feeling inferior to my brothers wasn't enough, I also had a best friend (one of three), Mark, who was ranked second in our class academically (and a fellow comic geek), which sometimes made it harder to deal with the fact that math and science didn't come naturally to me. I'd always been a decent student but not great. I liked English class but even then, I had trouble doing any kind of work that wasn't creative in nature (diagramming sentences, for instance, seemed to be the devil's work).

And speaking of the devil, three main factors were

bringing out the devil in my fifteen-year-old self. The first
and second were my other two best friends, Curtis and
Phil. Curtis was a senior, and we had already been friends
for about ten years, so we were close. Of course he brought
me to all of the senior parties. And of course I drank my
face off. That's what a fifteen-year-old is supposed to
do when he's invited to parties with eighteen-year-olds,
right?

No?

Well, anyway, Phil also liked to drink . . . and drink
we did. We smoked a ton of weed, too. Between those
two guys, I spent a lot of my sophomore year walking
around in a daze.

Which brought me into serious conflict with the third
factor:

My dad.

He's a big dude, over six feet tall (while I was probably
five and a half feet at most back then). He was physical
with me as a kid, as a lot of parents seemed to be back
then, and I was terrified of him. But when I turned fifteen, maybe because of the booze- and weed-fueled haze,
or maybe because it's what fifteen-year-old boys do with
their fathers as part of some kind of subconscious rite of
passage, I started fighting back. Not literally, because he
would have flattened me, but I ratcheted the attitude up
to eleven. I started talking back, something I had never
done before. I started lying about where I was. And I
started doing worse and worse in school. And acting like
I didn't give a damn.

This did not go over well.

The tension between me and my dad really began to escalate. And as if in response to our deteriorating relationship, the partying ramped up. The devil always gets his way. One night in particular seems to crystallize in my hazy memories of that year—the night that began the true downward spiral for me.

I was at Phil's house. We were drinking or smoking, or probably both, I'm sure, when cops showed up at the door. I remember getting scared that they were there to arrest us for the cannabis. But no, it was so much fucking worse than that.

Phil's mother had been killed in a car accident. I was standing next to my best friend when he found out that his mother had just died.

I can barely remember the rest of the night but I do know it was an anguished, gut-wrenching experience. I think I spent the night but I honestly don't even remember. I wish I did, but then again, maybe I'm glad I don't. Within a few months, he moved away, and while we stayed in touch, it was never really the same between us.

Meanwhile, my other best friend, Curtis, started to drift. Of course he did. I was fifteen. He was eighteen. How long did I really think he'd want a comic book–reading mascot dragging him down?

And as if all that wasn't enough, I got my first F ever (in math, naturally—geometry, the most evil branch of mathematics—why do I have to prove to you why a triangle is a triangle?!) and my dad hit the fucking roof. I remember being in the car at one point and for some reason he was in the backseat with me. We were in the parking lot of the local donut shop. I said something flip and it was like a switch went off and I saw his eyes glaze over in pure, unfiltered fury. He punched the seat in front of us so hard that the car shook.

I had hit rock bottom. The devil was winning.

But it's a devil that saved me.

In 1986, a small comic company named Comico published *Grendel: Devil by the Deed*, a graphic novel collecting short stories that had been appearing in the back of Matt Wagner's popular limited comic book series *Mage*. *Grendel* was the story of Hunter Rose, a socialite and novelist, who moonlights as a masked assassin. *Devil by the Deed* led to an ongoing *Grendel* series, the first story arc of which had a distinct impact on me. This particular story was entitled *The Devil's Legacy* and was the story of a female Grendel, Christine Spar, who avenges the murder of her son, Anson. You know, light stuff.

Most comic fans were crazy for *Mage* (which was pretty awesome, I have to admit) but *Grendel* was the comic that really captured my imagination. So much so that I took it upon myself one day to cobble together an all-black superhero costume and mask. And yes, I wore it. Outside. At night. Only once . . . but still.

Cloaked in shadows, I climbed my high school roof, clad in my superhero costume, and waited for a crime to occur on my watch (and this was way before *Kick Ass* and the awesome new *Daredevil* Netflix show, for the record).

What am I doing on this roof wearing a superhero costume? I thought, staring out through my mask into the inky darkness of my small Connecticut town, tensing for action.

Thank God I never witnessed a mugging—I probably would have been dumb enough to try to do something and would have been stabbed or shot repeatedly, or both.

(An even more embarrassing side note—in true Peter Parker–esque fashion, my mom found my costume—hidden, not very well—in the basement. She looked terrified when she confronted me with it, and when I told her what it was, a flood of relief washed over her face—apparently, she thought it was some sex thing. But I digress.)

So, yeah, I was into *Grendel* in a big way. The idea of wrestling the devil inside spoke to me, even if part of me knew I was losing the battle.

My grades were going down the toilet, I was estranged from my best friends, and my dad seemed ready to murder me. But you know what?

Grendel saved me.

Something else that happened to me in tenth grade is that I started writing short stories. I took my first-ever creative writing class, and once I'd written my first "real" story for that class (a total rip-off of Stephen King's first *Dark Tower* book), I was hooked.

One of my more pretentious stories (and that's saying something) was entitled "This World, This Society." Even though I have it somewhere in my basement, I don't even really remember what it was about. But at the time, I thought it was one of the greatest short stories ever written.

So much so that I sent it to Matt Wagner, my idol, the creator of the *Grendel* comic book. Now, remember, this was 1988. I mailed it to the comic book company, so I not only had no idea if Matt would read the story, I didn't even know if he would receive the damn thing.

Along with the story, I sent a pitch letter for a future *Grendel* storyline. I posited that Anson had actually survived having his eyeball eaten and could become the new one-eyed Grendel. I even included a drawing of the iconic Grendel mask, but with only one eye.

Weeks went by. I continued my spiraling behavior. And then, it arrived. A letter from Matt Wagner.

He had sent my story back to me, never a good sign. But then I flipped it over. On the back of the last page, he had written:

Your story is very good. Keep writing. Unfortunately, Anson is quite dead.

Those twelve words literally changed my life. Seriously.

They made me realize that I didn't have to be a jock, or be a great musician. I didn't have to drink or smoke to express myself to my peers (or to anyone else). I didn't have to be like anyone else at all. I could just do the thing that had always spoken to me: writing.

And so . . . I kept writing. After all, Matt Wagner told me to. I turned my grades around. I stopped with the weed and the alcohol (I mean, not completely . . . I'm human). I read *Grendel* by John Gardner, which changed my life, too. And it didn't stop there.

I wrote a book when I was eighteen (it was terrible). I went to college. I wrote my second novel when I was twenty-one (it was a little less terrible). I wrote a kid's book when I was twenty-five (it got produced as a play in New York City and got a great *New York Times* review). And my fourth book, the first one to get published, which I started writing in 1995, came out in 2014. When I first moved to New York, I started a production company called (of course) *Grendel's Mother Productions*. I've written *Flash Gordon* comic books, I wrote an *Island of Misfit Toys* graphic novel, and I'm now an editor at a major publishing company and I'm hard at work on my next novel and my next comic book and hopefully getting this essay finished in time. (If you're reading these words—guess what? I did it! Somehow.)

I don't think any of that would have been possible if I hadn't been obsessed with *Grendel* and if Matt Wagner hadn't sent me a twelve-word letter.

As for my dad and my three best friends from high school? I'm proud to say that my dad and I are extremely close now and we've worked through those issues. And hell, I have kids now and I can only imagine how frus-

trating I was for him! And I'm still good friends with
Mark, Curtis, and Phil, and see them whenever I can
(which isn't as often as I'd like).

So, yeah. The devil saved my life. Long live Grendel.

YOU NEVER FORGET YOUR FIRST TIME

NEIL GAIMAN

I've almost never written Batman, but he's what drew me into comics. I was six years old and my father mentioned that, in America, there was a *Batman* TV series. I asked what this was, and was told it was a series about a man who fought crime while dressed as a bat. My only experience of bats at this point was cricket bats, and I wondered how someone could convincingly dress as one of those. A year later the series began to be shown on English TV, and I was caught, as firmly and as effectively as if someone had put a hook through my cheek.

I bought—with my own pocket money—the paperback reprints of old *Batman* comics: two black-and-white panels to a page of Lew Sayre Schwartz and Dick Sprang, Batman fighting the Joker, the Riddler, the Penguin, and Catwoman (who had to share a book). I made my father buy me *SMASH!*, a weekly British comic that reprinted what I now suspect must have been an American *Batman* daily newspaper strip as its cover feature. I was once thrown out of our local newsagents— literally picked up by the proprietor and deposited on the sidewalk—for spending too much time examining each and every one of the pile of fifty American comics, in order to decide which Batman product would receive the benison of my shilling. ("No, wait!" I said, as they dragged me out. "I've decided!" but it was already too late.)

What got me every time was the covers. DC's editors were masters of the art of creating covers which proposed questions to mysteries that appeared to be insoluble. Why was Batman imprisoned in a giant red metal bat, from which not even Green Lantern could save him? Would Robin die at dawn? Was Superman really faster than the Flash? The stories tended to be disappointments, in their way—the question's sizzle was always tastier than the answer's steak.

You never forget your first time. In my case, the first-time *Batman* cover artist was Carmine Infantino, whose graceful lines, filled with a sly wit and ease, were a comfortable stepping-off point for a child besotted by the TV series. Text-heavy covers, all about relationships— Batman being tugged between two people: look at the first appearance of Poison Ivy (Will she ruin Batman and Robin's exclusive friendship? Of course not. Why did I even worry about such trifles?) looking here as if she's just escaped from the label of a tin of sweet corn. Batman thinks she's cute. Robin's not impressed. That was what I needed as a kid from a *Batman* cover. Bright colors. Reassurance.

While humans tend to be conservative, sticking with

what they like, children are *utterly* conservative: they want things as they were last week, which is the way the world has always been. The first time I saw Neal Adams's art was in *The Brave and the Bold* (I think it was a story called "But Bork Can Hurt You"). I read it but was unsure of whether or not I liked it: panels at odd angles, nighttime colors in strange shades of blue, and a Batman who wasn't quite the Batman I knew. He was thinner and odder and wrong.

Still, when I saw Adams's cover for "The Demon of Gothos Mansion!" (*Batman* 227), I knew that this was something special, and something *right*, and that the world had changed forever. Gothic literature tends to feature heroines, often in their nightdresses, running away from big old houses which always have, for reasons never adequately explained, one solitary light on in a top-floor room. Often the ladies run while holding candelabras. Here we have instead a dodgy-looking evil squire running after our heroine, between what look suspiciously like two wolves. The spectral, Robin-less, Batman is not swinging from anything. Instead he is a gray presence, hovering over the image: this tale is indeed a gothic, it tells us, and Batman is a gothic hero, or at least a gothic creature. I may only have been eleven, but I could tell gothic at a glance. (Although I wouldn't have known that the cover that Adams was intentionally echoing, *Detective Comics* 31, was also part of the gothic tradition—an evil villain called the Monk reminds the reader of Matthew "Monk" Lewis's novel, *The Monk*, and, as I learned a couple of years later, when the story was reprinted in a *DC 100 Page Super Spectacular*, the Monk from this story was a vampiric master of werewolves (or possibly vice versa, it's been a long time since I read it. I do remember that Batman opened the Monk's coffin at the end, and, using his gun—the only time I remember him using a gun—shot the becoffined Monk with a silver bullet, thus permanently confusing me as to the Monk's werewolfish or vampiric nature).

By the time I was twelve Len Wein and Bernie Wrightson's *Swamp Thing* was my favorite comic; it was, I think, the comic that made me want to write comics when I grew up. *Swamp Thing* 7, "Night of the Bat," was the comic that sealed Batman in my mind as a gothic figure. The cover only implies what's inside, as Batman, his cloak enormous behind him, swings toward the muck-encrusted swamp monster, inexplicably hanging from the side of a skyscraper. The feeling that this was something happening at night, artificially lit, in the city, was there, almost tangible. But the things that made me remember this cover fondly are really inside—Bernie drew Batman with no pretense of realism. It was as far as one could get from Adam West: behind Batman an unwearably long cloak blew out: Was it fifteen feet long? Twenty feet long? Fifty? And the ears, stabbing upward like devil horns, were even longer than Bob Kane's Batman ears on the cover of *Detective* 31. Wrightson's Batman was not a man—obviously: a man would have tripped over that cloak when he walked, the ears would have poked

holes in ceilings—he was part of the night. An abstract
concept. Gothic.

One of the greatest joys to the concept of Batman is that he isn't one thing, that he contains all the Batmans that have walked the streets of Gotham City in the last sixty-five years: Infantino's elegant Batman, Sprang and Schwartz's big gray Boy Scout, Frank Miller's Dark Knight. None of them more real, more valid, more true than any other. But in my heart, he is a spectral presence, a creature straight out of the gothic romances, and that, for me, is how he will always remain.

SUPERHEROES AND GENDER

WE ARE NOT AMAZONS

LEIGH BARDUGO

It began with a bustier. You can call it a breastplate if you like, but it began as a bustier—Vargas girl lingerie decked out in stars and stripes, a piece of clothing that gives new meaning to suspension of disbelief.

As a kid, eating bowls of cereal and watching *Super Friends,* I didn't question how Wonder Woman ran in heels or how she kept that red bustier from sneaking south. I put on my Wondy Underoos, made bulletproof bracelets from construction paper, and took to the back-yard to twirl with abandon, utterly transformed. When two girls showed up at a swim party in Wonder Woman bathing suits—as they invariably did—we didn't fret over the practicalities of fighting crime in your skivvies. We just argued over who got to be Wonder Woman and which poor sucker got stuck being Wonder Girl.

I lived on superhero stories in Saturday morning car-toons. I learned to spell with the *Super Friends* diction-ary. I adored Firestar in her skintight, flame-emblazoned onesie. In the evenings, I worshipped Lynda Carter as Wonder Woman, down to the rich click of her boots on whatever pavement she happened to be pounding. My favorite episode? The origin story of course, when Diana donned a blond wig and competed in secret to journey to the world of men. I graduated to comics, to Black Canary in fishnets and bolero, to Storm in her Mohawk and midriff-baring leathers. They were power and beauty, and when I was watching or flipping the pages, I walked among them as an equal.

Then, when I was ten, my camp counselor took me aside. Her name was Jill and, though she couldn't have been twenty, at the time she seemed wise, experienced, infinitely cool. She had red hair to her waist and drove a convertible. I didn't worry about being in trouble when Jill sat me down at a picnic table at the end of the day. I was a high-achieving kid, eager to please. I just assumed I was being singled out for something special.

"Listen," she said, voice gentle, raspberry gum cracking. "We think you need to have a talk with your mom about getting some new bras."

I didn't really take in her meaning at first. I just remember a full body cringe at hearing my mother and bras mentioned in the same sentence. Only later would I think on the awfulness of that "we," humiliation hitting in waves that never seemed to lose their force. *We think.* The idea of Jill and her friends trying to figure out a tactful way to raise the issue, deciding who would face the task of discussing it with me, all those older, cooler, effortless girls embarrassed on my behalf.

"Something with an underwire," she continued. Then

she gestured vaguely at my chest. "This is kind of out of control."

I wish my body had actually been out of control. Then I might have thrown up on her shoes or peed on the picnic table or spat my teeth out at her. Instead I just nodded, croaked, "Sure," and spent the rest of the day hunched over, desperate to be home, cursing the thin cotton of my rainbow T-shirt, wondering who was looking at me and what they saw. I rode the bus home with my knees drawn up to my chest, feeling every jounce in the road, every damning jiggle. *Out of control.* Apparently, my breasts required something more than a training bra to keep them in check. They were out of training. They had run amok and taken to the field.

I was never a nymph. I skipped the stage glorified by pervy old directors in artfully lit coming-of-age films. Puberty came on faster than a locomotive and I was helpless, tied to the tracks. Kids' clothing stopped fitting me correctly. My breasts had weight that caused the spaces between my blouse buttons to gap. Our perfectly respectable phys ed shorts rode high on my thick thighs. I was tall for my age, nearly five foot nine by the sixth grade. When I was twelve, I looked sixteen. When I was sixteen, I looked like a grad student. I got asked on my first date when I was ten. This didn't make me popular. It made me miserable in my own skin. It made me slouch. And it changed the way I looked at superheroes.

I bought my comics at a newsstand right near the

corner of Van Nuys and Ventura. It was wedged between a pizza place and a beauty supply called the Bee Hive where you could buy bottles of hair dye and cheap silver earrings. Back then, people still had to venture from their homes to buy their porn, so I had to walk past the girlie mags on the way to get the latest *X-Men*. I kept my shoulders hunched, wore baggy sweatshirts even at the height of the Southern California summer, and I stole glances at the partially hidden covers of *Playboy* and *Hustler* as I passed, as curious as I was self-conscious. I was fascinated by the models' big hair, heavy eye makeup, the halo of light that seemed to surround their airbrushed skin. They didn't look much different than the women in my comics, backs bent, chests thrust forward, full lips parted. Once I walked to the newsstand in my new pink Candies—faux leather with tiny heels and bows over the toes. "Those are sexy," said the guy at the register. I never went back.

Superheroes stopped making sense to me. Black Canary bound and lying on her side in her fishnets and heels wasn't glamorous anymore, she was vulnerable and about to be in serious danger. And Wonder Woman? I could barely stand to wear a swimsuit to the beach without covering it up with a long T-shirt. How was I supposed to stop mad scientists and megalomaniacs in one? What person, male or female, would choose to go into a fight as physically exposed as Wonder Woman? Where were her tights? Where were her *straps*? Looking at her didn't make me feel strong, it made me feel skeptical. Only an

Amazon could get away with that outfit. If some guy pulled up beside her in his car when she was walking to the mall, rolled his window down, asked her if she wanted to fuck, she wouldn't have to start looking for a store to duck into the way I did. She'd pull that guy right through the driver's side window and make him sorry. She'd crumple up his car like tissue paper. I was no Amazon. I was a girl whose body was *out of control.* I didn't want to be looked at. I didn't want to feel afraid.

I still loved heroes, but Wonder Woman and the supergirls of the comics panels lost their places to a bunch of upstarts in miniskirts. I gave my heart to Jem, She-Ra, Sailor Moon–type all-girl crews. Sure, they showed cleavage, wore heels, had ridiculously expressive hair, but at least they got to wear *skirts* instead of just panties in primary colors. They weren't contorted in the same breast-thrusting, booty-popping poses. They went on adventures, made friends, stopped evil, wore glitter at every opportunity, and had chaste romances with cute boys named Rio and harmless rogues like the Sea Hawk. They were female fantasies created for girls. I wasn't an Amazon, but maybe I could be a rock star who fought crime on the side.

Oddly enough, only Frank Miller's *The Dark Knight* slipped past the barricades. Or maybe it wasn't so strange. There, beside the caped crusader, was the sometimes maligned Carrie Kelley, flat chested and sporting an androgynous haircut—a girl fighting crime in an admittedly absurd outfit but unburdened by traditional visual indicators of femininity. She wasn't SomethingGirl or WhateverWoman. She was just Robin. I traced the images in those panels. I gave Carrie blond hair like mine. I didn't look like her. I hadn't looked like her for years and never would again, but she was what I needed to see—a girl devoid of powers, buoyed by nothing but Batcables and bravery, built for strength instead of sensuality. And do you know what else I found in those pages? Selina Kyle, aka Catwoman, thoroughly declawed—aged, wrinkled, turning tricks, beaten and left hogtied in a Wonder Woman costume, another body out of control.

It would be years before Wonder Woman and I met again, this time over a keg at a college Halloween party. By then, I'd gone full preppy—safe sweaters, collared shirts. My bras were serious architecture, buttresses, straps, masterpieces of restraint. I had dieted the worst of my shaming jiggle into submission. That night I was dressed as some vague undead thing—long black dress, hair in a tangle, red Solo cup in hand. I saw Catwoman first, Selina Kyle in top form, dressed in the shiny patchwork latex made legendary by Michelle Pfeiffer. She was dancing on her own, like a sleek black satellite. Then I saw her friend, Wonder Woman, walking slowly toward me. She was a tall brunette, gorgeous, dreamy, glassy-eyed drunk, wearing the classic Wonder Woman costume, little more than patriotic lingerie. *Jesus,* I thought, caught between scorn and envy, *really?*

It was a bit like seeing an ex. Why do you have to show up and ruin my good time? Why do you have to get me thinking about what it was like to love you? This was an ex I'd heard rumors about over the years. I'd heard the stories about how her creator, William Marston, was into bondage, how he'd lived with his wife and mistress and all of their children in some kind of love cult pre-hippie farmhouse. Her image turned up in unexpected places—on a women's studies syllabus that reproduced her striding across the cover of the first issue of *Ms. Magazine,* in a kitschy belt with a double-W buckle that I couldn't resist buying in a Seattle boutique but never wore. My response when Wonder Woman cropped up was never, "Oh, I remember her." It wasn't nostalgic fondness either. Wonder Woman was a part of my childhood, but I'd managed to leave most of the female characters of my childhood behind. I didn't give much thought to Scarlett or Lady Jaye from *G.I. Joe.* If I wanted to recall the glory of my wayward youth, I could crank up *Jem and the Holograms* and binge on madeleines. But Wonder Woman wasn't past. She was always present.

That night at the party, I felt all the things I'd felt when my own body turned on me. Catwoman I could admire. Wonder Woman set off something different inside me, something I didn't like. Looking at that fearless girl in satin, I had to ask why. The ex had returned and part of me hated her for betraying me, but part of me loved her still.

The girl in the costume was named Avery. We never

became friends but I watched her from afar. She was impossible to miss. She wore short skirts and knee-high boots. She made the college paper for simulating sex acts atop a table in a film studies class. She was outrageous in the most literal way. Her body was a means of protest and I began to understand that Wonder Woman costume had been a challenge. The impossibilities of Wonder Woman's costume were what had driven me away from her and other superheroines, but now they were what began to bring me back to her again.

Slowly but surely, Wonder Woman became my muse of audacity. She was the voice that whispered to buy the tight tank top, that choker that looked more like a dog collar than a necklace, those leather pants. She told me to cut my hair short and to dye it as red as her boots. She dared me to be unafraid to be seen. The next Halloween I went as the tattooed lady, bare arms and belly adorned with nothing but paint, a parade of lazy hand-drawn bees traveling up my cheek from the flowers on my neck as if seeking honey.

It's easier for us to conceive of a heroine in Black Widow's slinky but staid bodysuit or Batgirl's new yellow combat boots. But I think we need Wonder Woman in that bra, those bracelets, those bright, unapologetic colors precisely because they threw me for such a loop.

On any other woman, Wonder Woman's costume would be interpreted as an invitation to ogle, an opportunity to judge the wearer's intent, her psyche, even her morals. *Who does she think she is? What does she think she's doing?* Wonder Woman isn't subject to those same questions. She is free from the relentless "if she didn't want me to stare, she wouldn't have worn that" presumptions. Wonder Woman is a superhero. She came to fight. She came to win. She's going to do it in her uniform and her uniform happens to be shiny underwear. No one gets to misconstrue those star-spangled panties as an invitation to grab her Amazon ass.

I am not an Amazon. I don't have superstrength. I'm not even particularly fond of crunches. As I grow older, I find new judgments placed on my body: too big, too round, too soft. There are different pressures to keep myself covered, but they are the same voices of adolescence, the imagined Greek chorus chanting, *What was she thinking? Who does she think she is?* The way I dress is constrained by fear of judgment, by the need to code strength and professionalism in very particular ways, to comport with someone else's idea of respectability. But why should Wonder Woman, my fantasy of strength, be bound by mortal modesty? She is both soldier and pinup, both icon and eye candy.

I think often of Wonder Woman's bracelets. She has had numerous costumes over the years, but through almost every iteration, through bustiers and breastplates, through bottoms thick and thong, those bands of metal have remained—changing color and size, sometimes more bauble than bracer, but still retaining their purpose. In the mythology Marston built around those bracelets, Wonder Woman could only be robbed of her superstrength if they were chained together. And if she was freed of them, she would run amok, unstoppable, an Amazon unbound. I grew up afraid of what my body might do if freed, what attention it might garner, what shame it might bring. But for me, those bracelets have nothing to do with control or restraint. Instead, I see them for what they are: *armor*—the one functional bit of attire Wonder Woman retains on her vulnerable body. Those bracelets speak to what is most fundamentally resonant about Wonder Woman, because the act of walking around in your underwear—or a miniskirt and heels or long sleeves and sensible shoes—and trying to get the job done is actually something a lot of women understand.

When women dress, we walk the same line Wonder Woman has always walked, negotiating the same territory of the professional and the provocative. We are at once trying to honor the desire to choose our attire based on our own wants while still understanding the way our clothing is coded for those who observe us. We know that no matter how we dress or what our intent, our clothing will incite judgment and that we will invariably be measured against male fantasy.

We make these choices without the benefit of armor, and those bulletproof bracelets are something we all covet: a defensive weapon that can literally be used to turn a villain's attack back on him. They're the power of the ricochet, a perfect metaphorical refutation of the male gaze: "Whatever you send my way, I will give right back to you."

I'm a fantasy author now. I write female heroes. But the night of my book launch, as I try to decide what to wear, I feel the old fears set in. I will be photographed, tagged on Facebook, commented upon. I will be on display. I feel the shame of sitting at that picnic table with Jill, hear that chorus kick in, voices thick with pity and derision: *What was she thinking? Who does she think she is?* I could use restraint, silence my body, and make sure it sends no message at all rather than risk the wrong message. But I try to let Wonder Woman answer instead. I choose a short black dress, high platform wedges trimmed in gold like a lasso. My calves are emphatic. My hair is a yellow riot. With these choices, I don invisible bracelets. I am not an Amazon, but I might become one—fearsome, inviolable, bulletproof.

The first girl in my signing line is built the same way I was, the way I am, her belly overflowing the waist of her jeans, her T-shirt tight across her chest. "I love your dress," she says, beaming.

"Thanks," I reply as I settle my weight into the chair and cross my mighty thighs. "I love it, too."

WEAPON X

RON CURRIE, JR.

People always imagine that their time or generation is the "most" something or other. Right now, for example, there's no end to dinner table and twenty-four-hour-news-channel blather about how ours is the most politically contentious moment in American history, even though most of us have at least a glancing acquaintance with a moment in American history known as the Civil War. There exist, for another example, many misguided souls who believe LeBron James is the best basketball player of all time, despite ample one-click-away video evidence of the fact that Michael Jordan performed nightly miracles that even King James couldn't approach.

We've never been more connected. We've never been more alone. We've never been richer, nor poorer. It was the best of times, it was the worst of times. Et cetera, et cetera, ad nauseam.

We like to throw these assertions around because to say that our time is the "most" anything validates our basic narcissism, fools us into believing that we're not living just a minutely altered version of a life that's been lived billions of times before. It's all bunk, of course. History will repeat itself endlessly—or at least for as long as we're able to keep replicating our genetic codes on yet another successive generation, so that then, with our next breath, we can start grousing about how unprecedentedly spoiled they are.

All that said, I'm not above playing the game myself, so forthwith: there has never been a geekier time in contemporary American history than the 1980s.

There are innumerable nerdy totems I could cite to back up this contention, but I think the only thing I really need is the fact that the eighties were responsible for the *Revenge of the Nerds* franchise. Consider: we're talking about a moment so thick with geekdom that a series of movies starring Anthony Edwards and Curtis Armstrong became cultural touchstones. A *series* of movies. Not just one movie.

And in this time of intense and widespread competition for dork supremacy, I was a nerd among nerds. My dearest wish was to find a TRS-80 computer under the Christmas tree with my name on it, and when I did—how my parents ever afforded it I have no idea, but there it was—I immediately set about teaching myself how to program in BASIC and Pascal. By the time the first computer class rolled around, in junior high, I knew more than the teacher and spent the entire semester playing Zork while the rest of the students learned that a mouse was not just a small rodent, and I was proud, ridiculously, nerdtastically proud, to have distinguished

myself so completely from my classmates. In a nod to
my father's love for and skill at baseball, I suffered
through one season of Little League, striking out nearly
every at bat, bursting into inconsolable tears nearly every
time I struck out, and making solid contact only once, a
line drive straight at the shortstop, who a) was a girl,
and b) caught that shit. Having played Dungeons &
Dragons is considered entry-level bona fides for a geeky
childhood, but I didn't just *play* D&D, I *cheated* at it.
Constantly. That's how important it was to me. And I
and my (few) friends went well beyond D&D, losing
untold hours to Car Wars, Robotech, and Call of Cthulhu,
among others. All this, in addition to the hundreds of
books I lugged around and read at every opportunity—
in trees (no lie, literally *in trees*), in bed, on the bus, in
the bathtub.

And of course, some of those books were comics. Given
how my time and energy were spread out among so
many nerdy pursuits, I did not burn with a singular ded-
ication to the medium of capes and cowls; I was, in fact,
a bit of a dilettante, reading little beyond a few key series
and graphic novels: *Maus*, *The 'Nam*, a dalliance with
Love & Rockets that, had I possessed anything resem-
bling good taste at that age, would have gone on much
longer. But I did spend an absolute shitload of time at a
comic book store, nay one Comic Vault, so named because
it occupied a unit in my town's former post office which
housed the eponymous Diebold strong room. When
I say I spent a shitload of time there, I mean at least several

hours after school most weekdays, and often entire week-ends, for over five years. And though I wasn't apeshit for comic books like some kids I knew, and didn't have the money to collect them even if I had been, I did spend a lot of time walking the stacks at the Comic Vault and taking in the visual cacophony of covers. I was ashamed of my poverty, and shy besides, and so I did not often flip through the books, because to flip through them without buying was, in my mind, to demonstrate want-ing but being unable to have. Better to assume an air of casual, almost indifferent perusal and keep hidden the peculiarly fierce longing that these covers, and the stories they housed, inspired in me.

Even now I can easily conjure up in my mind's eye the images of those books I found most fascinating but never held in my hands, let alone owned or read. There's the smirking Guy Fawkes mask on the front of the trade paper edition of *V for Vendetta*; the iconic splash of blood across the smiley face's eye from *Watchmen*; and of course Batman, bulked up and pissed off, leaping through the air while silhouetted from behind by a lightning bolt on Frank Miller's *The Dark Knight Returns*.

But it was the cover of another Miller work that really seized me by the throat, occupying, as it did, the conver-gence of many of my preoccupations and enthusiasms at age twelve: righteous badassery, Ukiyo-e art, the nature of masculinity, ninja weapons, long odds, good and evil (and how they can commingle in one person). I'm talking, of course, about the collected *Wolverine* issues 1 through 4.

Unlike some of the things I thought unassailably cool as a kid, the cover of *Wolverine*'s first series has not been diminished by age or perspective. It's such an arresting image, still: our hero, claws deployed and wearing an expression of rapturous fury, locked in hand-to-hand with half a dozen ninja. His hair is swept up into a dual-peaked pompadour, the virility of which is matched only by its improbableness, and his trademark muttonchops flare raggedly from his jaw like the beard on a Scottie dog. The combat is so close that he's fairly buried in a tumble of assailants—their limbs and blades flog and flash, and they glare murderously from behind black veils. They're a formidable bunch, to be sure, but somehow we still know that they're seconds from death. And indeed, a closer examination of the image demonstrates that the ninja are already losing this fight. In the background a sword flies loose, its owner's hand flailing limp with death so recent he hasn't even hit the floor yet; facing us, another ninja has fallen into a sort of pincer move in Wolverine's left leg, his scowl just giving way to wide-eyed alarm. These guys are done for and they don't even know it yet. Listen: one of them has his *manriki,* a kind of chain weapon, wrapped several times around Wolverine's neck—but our hero is holding the last loop *between his teeth*, like a wild animal who is very, very pissed off at having been trapped. There are other, more subtle indications that things are not going the ninjas' way. For example, they are a homogeny of black and gray; Wolverine, by contrast, is an explosion of color, his hair that peculiar blue of the sky at dusk, his gloves and boots bloodred, and his pants bright yellow. Yeah, I said yellow. Only one other guy in the history of pop culture has ever made clothes the color of a banana seem anything but fey, and his name was Bruce Lee. Getting the picture yet?

He is absolutely feral, indestructible in his rage—but also, somehow, unmistakably human.

I stood there stricken. Because, see, sure, I was happy enough as a dweeb whose waking hours were taken up with binary code and sixteen-sided dice, but there was a different part of me, just beginning to stir itself awake, that wanted other things out of this life, things that were wholly incompatible with being a geek. And though what I stood looking at was fantasy, it nevertheless pointed in the direction that this nascent part of me wanted to go.

Not too long ago, everyone's favorite serial provocateur Camille Paglia executed one of her patented, gleeful cannonballs into hot water when she told the *Wall Street Journal* that "primary education does everything in its power to turn boys into neuters." This incendiary bomblet was part of a larger defense of olde-tyme masculinity, which, I think everyone would acknowledge, is right now about as fashionable as Velcro wallets. Paglia asserts that "PC gender politics" have created an environment in which men, particularly men in the upper middle class, have no outlets for their natural male energies other than Internet porn and sports talk radio, and cannot be honest with women about sex, or really anything, for fear of running afoul of the current feminist zeitgeist. She laments the loss of "models of manhood" and claims that American masculinity has been reduced to a pantomime of what we see on television and at the movies.

And though she's speaking in a sociopolitical environment that has very little time for considering the travails of men, she's not alone among high-profile feminists. Christina Hoff Sommers, herself an accomplished lightning rod, shares many of Paglia's opinions, in particular regarding the lack of traditional models of masculinity for boys to aspire to and the ways in which those models have been censored or "pathologized."

There may be something to this on a macrolevel, but the experience of this man, as a boy, leads me to believe that most of us don't require anything "manly" to aspire to. The impetus to be manly is innate, near I can tell, and switches on for many or most of us around the same age that we would no longer qualify to sing soprano in the Vienna Boys' Choir. Surely this timing is not a coincidence, and the fact of it has little or nothing to do with whether we have valid models of masculinity to emulate, any more than whether our balls drop is dependent on valid models of ball dropping. *Ha!* Acknowledge it or not, it just happens, folks, and it was happening to me, for sure, right around the time I first laid eyes on the magnificent, manly, hyperviolent cover of *Wolverine*.

I saw in Wolverine not inspiration to become something other than what I was, but rather confirmation of what I already knew I wanted to be.

Would it be overstating things, or otherwise foisting an unreasonable amount of cultural weight on a mere comic book character, to suggest that Wolverine might be the ideal for postfeminist men seeking a balanced masculinity? A masculinity that strives for goodness while acknowledging, and sometimes giving quarter to, the beast within? A masculinity capable of being gentle while retaining both the willingness and ability to hand someone a beating if he's got it coming? A masculinity that celebrates the talents and autonomy of women, yet also makes provisions for supporting and, if need be, protecting them?

Maybe it would be asking a bit much of a make-believe mutant who spends much of his time dressed in spandex, but if we're interested in reclaiming a manhood that eschews body waxing and macchiatos, we could do worse than to start with Weapon X.

Witness the opening scene of *Wolverine* 1–4, in which we find Logan climbing a sheer limestone face in the Canadian Rockies, in search of a rogue bear that's eaten two Mounties. He means to kill the bear; this is, as Wolverine notes, the thing he does best—killing. He mentions it with both pride and a tinge of regret, and it's this ambivalence that I found so appealing as a kid, and still find appealing today. I submit to you that Buddha was wrong, that all of life is not suffering but rather ambivalence, and a fully realized masculinity embraces this ambivalence. It acknowledges that there are unpleasant things that need constant doing, insists on an eminent capability of doing them, and regrets their necessity all at once. Most of us, of course, will never need to hunt down and kill a murderous grizzly, but consider a different scenario that any of us might find ourselves faced with: a cat has been run down and is dragging its broken, flattened lower half across the pavement, mewling pitiably, near death, no hope, just needless pain. A man sees the scope of its damage, intuits the hopelessness, and understands the animal needs to be put down immediately, that with each passing second during which he does not act, the sum total of agony in the world increases. A man accepts the paradox of mercy: that it sometimes feels, even appears, cruel. A man grabs a shovel, or else stands over the poor creature and raises his boot, does what needs doing. He doesn't feel good about it, except maybe long after the fact, when the sting, and then the ache, of having taken a life goes out of the experience. But here is the obligation, and if he is a man, he fulfills it.

This is Wolverine's obligation as well. Of course it's rendered somewhat simplistically, but that's part of the appeal. His inner landscape is craggy and complex, but the circumstances that engage it are not. There is a bear, and it's gone mad, has been killing people. And though

Wolverine loves the wild world, and the animals within it, though he in many ways feels a stronger kinship with them than with humans, he has an obligation. It's simple, and wrenching: he seeks the bear in its den, noting, with some regret, the bear's fear and confusion at being challenged on its own turf. The bear charges, not realizing it's completely overmatched, and with one swipe Wolverine cuts off its left arm, then laments that he couldn't end it without mutilating the animal. "I wish there was another way," he thinks, just before delivering the killing blow, "but there isn't."

As a kid I liked the pure badassery of the whole scene, but what I liked even more was the justice that followed: Wolverine finds an arrowhead coated with poison in the bear's hide. This is illegal but, worse, according to Wolverine's code, it's immoral, lazy, cowardly. The poison didn't kill the bear, it just drove it insane. Using the scent on the arrow as a guide, Wolverine spends several days tracking the hunter, until he finds him sitting at a bar in a nearby town. Wolverine opts first to inform the man that he needs to have a conversation with the Mounted Police. He's giving the guy a chance, though he doesn't really deserve one. Whereupon the man slams a beer glass into his face. And Wolverine says, "I was hopin' you'd do somethin' like that."

It raises, for me, the question of how much we should tolerate before violence becomes an option. I've long been of the opinion that being "the bigger man" and walking away, either from an overt challenge or a situation in which one person is ruining the vibe for many people, is often bullshit, the nonsense message of a culture that has fashioned an environment as consequence free for troublemakers and shit talkers as any Internet comments section. Again, the scenario in *Wolverine* is extreme, but there are parallels that most of us face in everyday life—the serial asshole at your local who has a habit of carrying on in a way that annoys everyone in earshot; the guy down the street who you spy grabbing his girlfriend roughly outside their front door. What's a man to do? A man asks the serial asshole to keep it down. A man stops and tells the guy to let the woman go. In these situations, a man may be invited to "make" the offender heed the request, in which case I'm reminded of a quote from an essay by Chris Jones entitled "In Defense of the Fistfight": "I would submit, Your Honor, that if someone is doing something demonstrably asinine, and I ask them to stop it, please, and they say, 'Make us,' they've entered a binding oral contract whereby I am permitted, even obligated, to try to make them."

Understand, this is not a call for throwing the first punch but of reserving the right to throw a punch if the situation ultimately calls for it, a right that I would argue has largely been taken from us. Note that Wolverine gives the man, who has something to answer for, a chance to cooperate. The man chooses otherwise, at which point Wolverine is justified in withdrawing the chance he's offered and substituting, in its place, an ass kicking.

Fistfights: they are almost always ultimately harmless, so long as no one's got a blade or a gun—a split lip here, a swollen eye there—but they serve to settle matters that prove insoluble with words. Someone ends up on his back, bleeding from the nose and gasping for air but unharmed in any significant way, and the problem has been settled. This is what men do. Or at least it's what they should do, what they used to do, before someone convinced us that this is not an important part of our nature.

Admit it—you've walked away from a fight once or twice, for whatever reason. Maybe you were plain scared or, worse, bought into the admonishments of polite white American culture: fighting is stupid. It never solves anything. No matter the circumstances, you will be judged poorly. And then you went home and felt that burning in your gut, the same burning you feel when you think of the perfect retort hours after an argument has ended. This could have happened years, decades ago—and yet, when it springs to mind, you still feel the burning. And it's my contention that this burning, which is really molten shame, is not nothing. It's not worth enduring for the sake of a misguided sense of propriety. It's toxic. In large enough doses, it can cripple you. And avoiding that shame is, in itself, good enough reason to fight. Even if you get your ass kicked, at least you'll be able to look yourself in the mirror the next morning.

Wolverine, friends, has never walked away from a

fight. He'd sooner run himself through with his own
blades.

But I had, standing there at the Comic Vault. I'd
walked—and in some cases run—from scraps with other
kids, at school, in the neighborhood. In case the reader
hasn't gathered from the previous descriptions of my
twelve-year-old self, I was a sissy. No two ways about it.

Does that seem a harsh assessment, especially for a
grown man to level at a barely adolescent boy? Maybe.
But consider two things:

1) It's unassailably true (remember, I cried at Little League
games, among many other things I haven't told you about).

2) The very context I'm asking you to reconsider—what
George Carlin referred to as "the pussification of the
American male"—is in large part what makes this dim
view of my childhood self seem harsh in the first place. In a
different, more honest time, many people would agree that
a kid for whom weeping is the default response to misfortune
and failure could probably use some toughening up.

As it stood, though, if any toughening up were to take
place, it was on me to make it happen. And I was ready.
I'd known for a while that I needed things to be different. At the time I would have articulated this desire in
superficial terms: I wanted more friends. I wanted the
interest of girls, those previously sexless classmates whose
attentions suddenly mattered a great deal. I wanted to be

a better athlete. I wanted to no longer be afraid of J. J. Beaulieu. This was how I articulated my motivations to myself. But these things were, of course, merely the byproduct of my real aims: strength of body and character. Courage. Capableness. Self-regard. Seriousness of intent. Stamina both physical and mental. Control—over myself and over the external events that swirled closest to my orbit.

As with Wolverine's skeleton, coated with adamantium to render it nearly indestructible, the first step, it seemed to me, was building up my body. I'd always been scrawny, one of those kids who if you put him in a dark room and pressed a flashlight to his belly, you'd be treated to an instant anatomy lesson, but being scrawny meant only that there was something to build on, nothing to eliminate.

So what to do? Hit the road and hit the weights, naturally. One of the mixed blessings of my life has been a singular, almost obsessive focus on the things I've set my mind to. Doesn't matter what it is—could be writing a book, could be drinking whiskey—if I'm doing it, I'm doing it all the way. And so it was with training. Once I started, and started to feel my body change, I was hooked, borderline obsessive. I exercised with a frequency and intensity that would cause adults today to worry about my growth being stunted, running until I puked, hoisting weights until my nose bled. I knew in the abstract that I was growing stronger—even exponentially stronger—but for a while there was no opportunity to test this in any practical way, in part because despite my burgeoning strength, I was still scared.

Meanwhile, look at Wolverine—after dispatching the bear and the poacher, he's now traveled to Japan to find his beloved, a woman named Mariko who has suddenly and without explanation started returning his letters and refusing his phone calls. Mariko's is an ancient and noble Japanese family, and Wolverine knows that, as an interloping gaijin, he'll be getting himself into a good deal of trouble and danger by pursuing her. But he doesn't care, first because he's a romantic and believes in the primacy of love and second because his principles have been offended, and one of those principles dictates that no amount of danger justifies abandoning one's principles.

I, too, was a romantic, in that exceedingly painful adolescent way. And I wanted to be principled enough to not back off my principles because of fear. Unlike saccharine romantic notions, though, that was a slightly tougher nut for me.

But eventually it happened, in a way that at the time seemed accidental, impulsive, but in fact could never have occurred if I hadn't spent the previous year building myself up and spending a great deal of mental energy pondering principle, courage, the kind of man I wanted to grow into. If not for that, I would have run just like before. This time, though, I made a different choice, one that informed everything that followed.

It happened at a junior high dance. Or rather outside the dance, in the parking lot of the YMCA. Probably a hundred and fifty kids had gathered there, waiting for the doors to open. One of those kids was me. Another was a guy named Larry Baker, a hulking eighth grader whose sheer mass was enough to terrorize most boys our age. At thirteen Larry had stubble that would have put George Michael to shame, and was already a grown man in pretty much every regard (except for the fact that he had the same ten-cent head as any other adolescent boy). He enjoyed his size, did Larry; had developed a bullying streak to accompany it; and was, in addition, on this particular night, screaming drunk.

In the parking lot the other kids had formed a large circle around Larry, and he reeled about its circumference, menacing anyone nearby with one canned-ham fist. Every time he approached the edge of the crowd it expanded outward, like a balloon being squeezed, and the kids, laughing nervously, scrabbled over one another to get away from him. Thus satisfied that his preeminence had been respected, Larry would lurch away and repeat this process with another section of the circle.

Judging by their reactions, many of the other kids found Larry's antics amusing. I didn't. The guy had all the intellectual capacity of a bulldozer, and then, as now, I did not suffer idiots well. So I made my way to the edge of the crowd and waited for him to come toward me, determined that, unlike everybody else, I would not run away.

I didn't entirely understand this decision, or even recognize it as my own. It was as though the me that I knew well had been hijacked by someone slightly braver, slightly more principled, and slightly more stubborn.

It didn't take long for the resolve of this new Ron to be tested. Here Larry came, his stupid pig's eyes bleary with booze, and as everyone scattered, those eyes fixed on me, widening with surprise and excitement. If I'd had more time to think about what was happening, I might have bolted, but the whole thing took maybe four seconds. Larry picked up speed, meaning it now, a berserker charge, and launched that fist straight at my face.

I felt the impact, a dull, painless thump, and saw a tremendous flash of white light. For a few moments I had no idea what had happened. But when my head cleared, I had a couple of important realizations. First, I was fine. I'd been punched square in the face by the biggest guy around, and not only did I not die—or shit my pants or any of the other things I always imagined would happen if someone clocked me—but I'd kept my feet. There was nothing wrong at all. What had I been so afraid of? Second, I was shaking, but these were not the impotent tremors of cowardice. This was the vibration of stored energy—that phenomenon I'd been learning about in science class—agitating for release. I was angry. Angry that this pituitary case was able to terrorize an entire group of us with impunity. Angry that he'd tuned me up for having the audacity to refuse to flee at his approach. Angry that guys like Larry Baker had their fucked-up worldview reinforced over and over by the simple fact that they kept getting away with treating people like shit.

And what a relief, to feel anger! To be rageful was to be alive, potent, *actual*. The paradox, for those who choose to fight Wolverine, is that when you hurt him, he grows furious and thus more lethal. Now that I'd been tested, it seemed I shared that quality.

And that was, for the moment, enough. I didn't go after Larry—I was angry, not stupid—and somehow, among my classmates, simply having stood my ground garnered me a sudden cachet. No one really said anything, but I could feel it in the way they looked at me. I was the dude who refused to run when everyone else was looking for cover.

More important, I'd earned a good deal of self-respect in the bargain. If I had fled, I would have left the dance that night unmarked but then spent the next several nights kicking the covers, burning in my gut, wrestling shame. Not now. Now I checked my face in the bathroom mirror, noted the swelling and bruising with satisfaction, and slept the sleep of a young man at ease with himself.

And I would learn, over the years, that being at ease with oneself really has little to do with whether or not you win a fight. Sure, it feels good to win. I'd be lying if I said I didn't enjoy the first time my new strength was tested and I tossed an older guy who used to torment me to the ground, giving him a bad enough pounding that my father came running down the street to intervene. But not even Wolverine wins every time. In fact, Wolverine actually loses, and loses badly, quite often for a superhero. Shingen, Mariko's corrupt, criminal father, beats the crap out of him with a wooden practice sword, then leaves him for dead on a Tokyo street corner. A samurai nearly kills him with one swipe of a katana; if not for Wolverine's adamantium bones, he would have been cleaved in half. At one point, he's even knocked out by Yukio, a woman whom he takes up with after Mariko breaks his heart. Wolverine gets his ass kicked over and over again, but as he succinctly puts it later in the story, "The key isn't winning—or losing. It's making the attempt."

If this seems reductive, well, most genuine truths do. And I'm not interested in a more complex or nuanced assessment. I understand that there exist exceptions to every rule, that there are plenty of men who by inborn temperament have no interest in fighting (or even verbal combat), that there are means of conflict resolution that don't involve a rough slow dance between two guys, and further that men do not have a monopoly on physical aggression. None of those things, which are facts, undercuts my extremely basic premise, the simple truth I know in my very bones, to wit: men fight. Not to the exclusion of women; women can fight all they like, if that's what they fancy. But this is not a discussion of gender relations, it's a simple statement: men fight. It's in our DNA, and to try to deny it, or turn it off, results in an incomplete man: not a neuter, exactly, but something less than what he would be otherwise.

But of course it must be tempered. Like Wolverine, we've got to struggle against our animal selves. We can't be running around the streets punching one another over bullshit. A willingness to fight is essential in a man, but just as essential is a well-honed acumen for knowing when a fight is not actually indicated. Here, admittedly, Wolverine struggles a bit, his attempt to let the poacher make the right decision notwithstanding. The truth is, the guy's always itching for a scrap. Me, I've sidestepped many more fights than I've engaged in. One incident not too long ago springs to mind: a guy who I knew in an extremely tangential way was hammered, and got the (completely wrong) impression that I was pushing up on his girlfriend. He came after me, all 140 pounds of him, right in my face, threatening to relieve me of my teeth if I didn't vacate the premises (which happened, fortunately, to be his house; if we'd been on neutral ground—a bar, for example—I would have told him to get fucked, and the incident probably would have escalated further). He was utterly and completely out of line, which his friends knew. They kept getting in his way and apologizing to me over their shoulders. All the while I held my hands up in a gesture of appeasement, backing out of the house and assuring him, with great good cheer, that

all was well. I didn't want to fight him for a number of
reasons, not least because the whole thing was too stupid to bear, but also because it simply wouldn't have
been sporting. This dude was built like a sheet of crepe
paper and no fighter besides, and while I'm not the biggest guy around, I did have seventy or so pounds on
him. If it had come to blows, he would have been in very
bad shape, but he didn't have the good sense to realize
that, and so it was on me to make sure no one got hurt.

All this is a way of saying a man has to trust himself.
If he's following his conscience as well as his pride, in
the end there will be little that he needs to apologize for,
even if cultural mores run counter to his instincts, his
sense of obligation to himself. And here's where Wolverine comes in again. Because of circumstances beyond
his control, he's basically spent the entire story doing
things that lost him Mariko's affection. Shingen sets him
up and makes it appear as if Wolverine is trying to murder him, instead of the other way around. Later, when a
troop of samurai makes an attempt on Mariko's life,
Wolverine goes berserk, losing himself completely in the
fight, and Mariko, never having seen that side of him, is
horrified. Then, at the end, Wolverine duels Shingen
once more, this time killing him in front of Mariko.
He's persisted through the loss of her love, doing what
he knew was right despite what it cost him. Comic
books being comic books, Mariko has by now realized
that her father brought shame to her family, and had

planned to kill Shingen herself if Wolverine had failed. But this is where comic books and life diverge, and a man sometimes has to be satisfied with a quiet conscience and a restful night's sleep. In a world such as ours, this is no small thing.

WONDER WOMAN

JODI PICOULT

When DC Comics approached me to write several issues of the *Wonder Woman* comic book series, my first order of business was to get that poor girl a functional outfit. After all, any woman who is even marginally as well-endowed as Wonder Woman knows you can't fight crime—much less go about more mundane daily activities—while you're worried about your top falling off. I had visions of her off panel, tugging up that glittery spandex corset. "Could we just add some straps to her bustier?" I asked, and I was politely told that the costume had been around for sixty-odd years for good reason.

It begged the question though: Why *has* Wonder Woman had such staying power? And for that matter, who's reading her? She has long been upheld as a role model for young girls—the epitome of a strong female icon—but her sheer bodaciousness (and that costume) suggests that it's her body, not her face, that's attracting male readers. The paradox began back in 1941, when she was created by William Moulton Marston—the psychologist who'd invented the polygraph. He believed that women were more honest than men and were better workers—and he had a vision of the future in which women ruled over men. As if this wasn't revolutionary enough for the 1940s, he and his wife, Elizabeth, lived with another woman, Olive Byrne, in a polyamorous relationship. His Wonder Woman was an amalgamation of the women in his life—free-spirited, unconventional, and strong. Known as Princess Diana to the Amazons with whom she grew up, Wonder Woman sported indestructible bracelets—a gift from Athena, and a lasso of truth—an Olympian deity's equivalent of Marston's polygraph. She was six feet tall, stunning, packed a mean punch—and slipped neatly into the Golden Age of comic books, when DC was powered by a testosterone triumvirate: Batman, Green Lantern, and Superman.

Believe it or not, girls used to read more comics than boys. In the early 1940s the Archie Comics and others like them offered three female role models: career girls who became nurses or secretaries; swooning heroines who got married and had happily-ever-afters; or bubblegum teens, like Betty and Veronica, who had catfights over Archie. Wonder Woman blew these stereotypes away. She was strong enough to kick Superman's ass; didn't need a guy to be happy; and had a job track that, in one of Marston's stories, took her right into the Oval Office as president of the United States. And yet, even as Wonder Woman battled the Nazis and crime, there were episodes of bondage that were at best cringeworthy and at worst the stuff of Marston's sexual fantasies. She became the first female member of the Justice League of America—but she was relegated to the role of secretary.

And that, really, is the paradox of Wonder Woman. As she's evolved, it's always been one step forward, two steps back. Why? Well, I have a theory. For sixty years, the adventures of the world's most recognizable super-heroine have been written by men. With the exception of a three-issue run by Mindy Newell in the 1980s, I was the first woman approached to write the Wonder Woman comic book series. Granted, some of the story lines created by the men were fantastic—but they also involved stripping Wonder Woman of her powers, dumb-ing her down to run a boutique, leaving her blind and bound. What's the point of having the world's strongest female superhero, if you're always trying to break her? It may have less to do with Wonder Woman herself than her male readers. When confronted by a strong, smart, beautiful woman, most guys are entranced . . . and a little bit terrified. It's one thing to say women are equal to men . . . it's another to suggest that women are *superior*. This is why Wonder Woman can't catch a break, even though she technically qualifies for a senior citizen ticket at the movies. She's allowed to be strong. She just can't be too strong—because then she alienates female readers, who find her too tough to identify with, and male readers, who find her too threatening to lust after.

Because she's walking such a fine line, Wonder Woman has always struggled to find an audience. Not surpris-ingly, she has a huge gay and lesbian following. Like her buddies Batman and Superman, whose male readers want to *be* them, Wonder Woman has always had female fans who admire her strength and her intelligence. But she has male readers, too, who admire—well—her breasts. As a writer, was there a way to keep both groups satisfied? I thought the answer, ironically, involved making Wonder Woman a little more like the rest of us. She'd still have all her superhuman powers—and her curves. But I didn't want to humiliate her—the least I could do, as a fellow female. In my story line, Wonder Woman was smarter than everyone else. *She* was the one who rescued the dude in distress. And I played up elements of her life that allowed female readers to relate to her in a visceral way they never had. Unlike Superman, who has a backstory in the real world (Clark Kent), Diana has always been an outsider. She loves humans, but she's never going to be one of them. Just like today's "wonder women," she has to do it all—balance work, family, and self—while secretly wondering every now and then, *Am I doing a good enough job?* In other words, Wonder Woman was vulnerable—not physically, like in those creepy earlier incarnations of bondage—but mentally, with doubts that seemed real, honest, and awfully human. Suddenly, Wonder Woman had enough of a chink in her armor to make a male reader feel like he was on equal terms. And for female readers, Wonder Woman's crisis of faith made her more than a sex symbol populating the fantasies of men. She was a *sister*; she was struggling; she was one of us.

I'm happy to say that I think Wonder Woman is headed in the right direction. In her current incarnation, she remains strong enough to go mano a mano with Superman, and she has incredible stamina. She's got experience fighting crime, political oppression, and sheer sorcery. She can communicate with all sorts of animals and has staggering wisdom. She's a flawless diplomat, leader, and warrior. And of course she still has that lasso of truth, to keep the rest of us honest. In fact, she sounds so much like real women I know that it's tempting to wonder whether life's imitating art or vice versa. And while having a Wonder Woman in the White House temporarily remains the stuff of legend, I'm delighted that for the first time ever, DC Comics assigned a female writer for a long-term run—the incredibly talented Gail Simone. Given that Ms. Simone was the impetus behind a website called Women in Refrigerators—a list of the gratuitous deaths of female characters in comic books, usually as a plot device for the male characters—I think Wonder Woman's in very good hands.

As long as little girls dress up in those red boots and a tiara for Halloween, as long as we all hope for good to triumph over evil, there's always going to be a place for Wonder Woman. Whether you admire her because she can kick through a brick wall without messing up her hair, or because she can (literally) fly circles around the guys, she represents what we all know: absolutely nothing can stand in the way of a strong woman.

In the last issue I wrote for DC Comics, I wrote

myself into the script, instructing the illustrator to make an Amazon warrior look like a certain red-haired novelist moonlighting as a comic book writer. And sure enough, when the issue hit the stands, there was my alter ego . . . systematically beating the crap out of Batman.

Just for the record: the breastplate of *my* armor had straps.

SUPERHEROES

AND CHILDHOOD

GOD OF THUNDER

KEVIN SECCIA

For as long as I can remember, I've been dispropor-
tionately concerned with one question:

"Who could beat up who?"

Could Spider-Man beat up Superman? Could the
Dark Knight pummel the Hulk? Could Paste-Pot Pete
stop Stilt-Man? (Yes, no, and I forget.)

When I was a kid, this was all brought to life in a
series of month-long debates focusing on two or more
entities and which among them was the toughest. In
the town of Vernon, New Jersey, where I grew up, the
answer to that question was "not me."

To elaborate, I was a skinny, asthmatic allergy suf-
ferer, and thanks to my half-Asian heritage, I looked
different from most of the kids in my neighborhood. I
didn't care for exercise, hated sports, and was even
awarded a special pass from the school nurse that allowed me to walk during the daily run in gym class (the
pass wasn't pink and ringed with delicate lace, but it
probably should have been). Give each of these qualities
to a single kid and you have the equivalent of throwing
snake eyes in the craps game that is growing up in the

suburbs of New Jersey. Not familiar with craps? Pick whatever sport or activity you enjoy the most and then fill in the worst thing that could happen to you in the middle of it. Baseball? Strikeout. Boxing? Knockout. Picnic? Thunderstorm.

I knew I could never be the fastest or most powerful, but the next best thing was reading about the guy who was.

In the Marvel comic book universe, the answer to this all-important question was Thor. He was the biggest, strongest, toughest character Marvel had. Thor was the only superhero who also happened to be a living, breathing god. Not some guy with a few bucks to blow on a grappling hook and a pair of shiny red boots. Not some goof who stumbled into the rays of an exploding comet on St. Patrick's Day, thus acquiring the power to get drunk and sweat green glitter. No, this guy was an immortal. An actual god of Norse mythology. Someone you could plausibly study in your history class.

(Full disclosure: There were maybe two other characters stomping around Marvel at that time with a claim on being able to beat Thor in a brawl. The Incredible Hulk, who was a moron and thus clearly inferior to a god, and a charisma-deficient alien known as the Silver Surfer who didn't even have his own comic book so, honestly, why are we even talking about him?)

Thor was the first hero I ever had. One day, out of the blue, he just was. I didn't pick him from a lineup of dozens of other heroes, who were devastated at having been rejected and then headed off to an afternoon of glum reflection and self-appraisal. ("Why didn't that geek pick me?! I wield fire!") All I remember is that one day Thor was my favorite. From that point forward I lived and died based on the results of his fictional exploits, hanging on every star-shattering punch. In hindsight, it makes a lot of sense.

Part of Thor's appeal was his simplicity. Spider-Man had the proportional strength and speed of a spider, as well as a "spider-sense" alarm, which alerted him to potential danger, and spider-silk-throwing web shooters, which ensnared bad guys. On the other hand, Thor was a humongous savage with a giant hammer.

Batman was a tactical genius, adept at sussing out your weaknesses days before a fight, capable of tracking you down, divining your motives with a detective's brain, and then defeating you with strategies that would favor his strengths and target you where you were most vulnerable. Thor would walk up to you and attempt to wallop you with his giant hammer. That was Thor's plan A, B, C, D, and X for stopping villains. You have to admire that.

Thor also seemed far more relaxed than your typical Marvel hero. Spider-Man was an angst-filled ball of dread, Captain America was a hard-assed disciplinarian, and Tony Stark had to hit the bottle just to keep the demons in check. Thor? Not a care in the world. I guess that's one of the added benefits of being a living god. You're pretty cool about shit.

Now, the hammer . . . one of the best things about the

hammer, in addition to the fact that it was a nearly un-breakable weapon of incalculable power and might, was that you could lift it only if you were worthy.

That's huge.

Think about the pressure and responsibility that would come with wielding, say, some nuclear-bullet-shooting machine gun. You'd be invincible on the battlefield, but then what? The moment you went to sleep, someone would steal it. You'd have to carry it with you 24/7, con-stantly doing that thing where you instinctively grab for it, the way you tap your back pocket checking for your wallet. It would turn into an obsession. You'd be like Gollum within a week.

And if it went missing, you'd have to live with the knowledge that some disgruntled teenager stole it and shot up a food court somewhere. Not Thor. He just sets that thing down anywhere he pleases. If he has to hit the restroom at the mall of Asgard and feels weird (justifiably so) about lugging the hammer into the john, he can just set it down outside. We have this particular enchantment to thank for Thor's calm demeanor and laid-back vibe.

But he wasn't perfect. Like most great heroes, Thor had a secret identity. And his was terrible. Thor's civil-ian persona was that of a frail doctor named Donald Blake. One day, after being ambushed by rock men from Saturn—as we've all had happen at one time or another—Blake found himself trapped in a cave, and in that cave he discovered a simple wooden cane. And when he struck that cane on the ground, he was instantly transformed into a six-foot-tall nearly invulnerable thunder god. And the cane was transformed into the hammer Mjolnir, an invincible weapon of limitless power. Yeah! That's it, right? A rent-controlled apartment on the proverbial easy street for ole Don?

Actually, no.

Unlike Superman, who dressed up as Clark Kent, Blake wasn't Thor in disguise. Blake actually *transformed* into Thor—an entirely different being—and they shared separate minds and experiences. In fact, Blake had no memory of what Thor said or did after he changed back. I don't know about you, but to me that sounds like a humongous rip-off. It sounds less like being a superhero and a lot more like being roommates with a superhero— one who never lets you tag along, who comes in late smiling some mile-wide shit-eating grin that only hints at the things he's seen and done, who constantly has women over who barely look at you, and who everyone always asks you about.

"Hey, Don! Thor saved my dad! What a champion! . . . So, you're, like, him?"

"Hah, oh, no. I just hang out, waiting for danger to arrive, and when it does I leave and he shows up."

The first person in the above conversation walked away when Don got to the word no.

Later ill-advised variations on Thor's alter ego had him going the more traditional secret-identity route, posing as a construction worker, Sigurd Jarlson. Sigurd was

Thor dressed in bell-bottomed jeans and goofy glasses, wearing his hair in a ponytail. I'm not sure why any of this day job stuff was necessary, considering a hunk of enchanted Norse gold would have set him up financially for a few hundred Earth years. Maybe Marvel Comics wanted to nail down the blue-collar comic-buying demographic, who'd ordinarily be turned off by some guy calling himself a god. Thankfully, this was just a phase.

So far I bet Thor sounds pretty great. An awesome, ass-kicking, name-taking superhero . . . an excellent candidate for your "favorite character," maybe? Well, hold on a sec.

It wasn't easy liking Thor. Standing up as some gawky, middle school kid and saying, "Thor's my favorite!" was what truly separated the men from the boys. Or, to be more accurate, the boys from the boys the first group of boys beats up.

Anyone can like Ghost Rider—a motorcycle-riding, leather-jacketed tough guy with a flaming skull for a head. Oh, and he's also covered in spikes. (C'mon! At this point why not make him part dinosaur and have one of his powers be "cutting school." We get it: he's awesome.)

Or how about the Punisher, a guy with a skull on his shirt, whose power is smirking while shooting guns? Or the Hulk, the guy who gets angry and hits things?

They aren't tough favorite characters to support. People tend to get onboard—even jocks. But try telling people you like the character with the luxurious mane of flowing blond hair, the guy who also wears a silver helmet with wings on it, who talks in old-timey Norse speak, littered with "thou" and "thus" and "verily." Classmates who already watched you with a wary eye will quickly come forward to call out your sanity, gender, and sexual preference. I mean, liking *any* comic book character wasn't really going to vault you into the social hierarchy—not to any spot you wanted to be in. But naming Thor as your favorite character was like dousing that spot with gasoline and sparklers.

So, why Thor?

This is the main reason, as far as I can tell. A reason more important than a laid-back demeanor and a cool weapon and the fact that he was—all due apologies to the Hulk—clearly the "strongest one there is." Because eventually all of that faded. The more I read of Thor's adventures, the more he'd win and the more he'd lose, and that ended up mattering less and less. What continued to matter was that he kept going—and kept fighting—regardless.

Here's the thing. He didn't have to. He didn't have to be here. It was almost wrong for him to be here—but there he was. I mean, Captain America was a guy fighting for his own country. Iron Man was a human—albeit one with a superpowered suit of armor—fighting to defend humanity against evil. They were human and it made sense that they fought for their planet and for other humans. They kind of had to. But Thor didn't. He didn't even seem to belong. They'd be sitting around Avengers

Mansion, waiting for some new disaster to strike, and Thor was above that kind of behavior.

He actually chose to be here, chose to try to make a difference, and honestly, as a frail, asthmatic kid, "here" was the last place I wanted to be. But if Thor, a god who could soar across the galaxy or be off fighting frost giants and bedding women while hefting flagons of mead . . . if he chose to be here, maybe here was okay.

Of course, he was wrong, but I didn't find that out until years later. His heroics prevented me from becoming a jaded, world-weary man years before my time, and that's no easy task. He saw a nobility in mankind that wasn't on display in the halls of northern New Jersey's Lounsberry Hollow Middle School. At the time, it was enough.

Eventually, I moved on to other heroes: boxers, Steve McQueen, even my own father, but the scion of Asgard himself, Thor, the god of thunder, was the first. And anyone who says he's not the strongest hero of all time— that he couldn't mop the floor with Superman—is a damn, dirty liar.

UNDERDOG AND ME

MARTIN KIHN

What happens when criminals in this world appear and break the laws that they should fear? Well, here's what, bitches:

> *The cry goes up from far and near*
> *for Underdog! Underdog!*

Starring that "champion of champions," the pill-popping supercanine who isn't really a dog and is certainly no underdog, humbly underselling his labor as alter ego Shoe Shine Boy for five cents—even in the mid-1960s, when the show started, a nostalgic price—and sniffing around after an accident-prone diva named Sweet Polly Purebred, who isn't all that sweet and is certainly no purebred.

Yep, there's a lot going on in . . .

The Underdog Show—Part 1

As a kid growing up on the far right side of the right side of the tracks in Bloomfield Hills, Michigan, which sounds exactly as white as it is, the *Underdog* show was the only television program I was allowed to watch. Those of you with normal childhoods will find this hard to believe. I don't mean *Underdog* was the only show I was allowed to watch on Saturday morning or allowed to watch when I was acting up: I mean *allowed to watch ever.*

Until *The Love Boat* became my family's regular Saturday night cruise into forced intimacy, my little brother and I were exposed to *Underdog,* and *Underdog* alone.

Why? Quite simple, really: my parents are Scottish and South African snobs. Ex–British Empire colonials don't appreciate much, but they do like irony. To this day, the units have refused to naturalize; they despise American culture, distrust television's deeper motives. My grandmother, a pint-sized Glaswegian with thick bottle-lensed glasses, informed my mum around 1959 that she could get "square eyes" from looking at the tube. This is what passed for pop culture wisdom in our house. My mum was an epic reader, a literary critic, yet there was something she liked very much about *Underdog.* The show is shockingly literate, paws-itively clever.

The superdog's manners didn't hurt. He had the kind of between-the-wars diffidence we find today only in Minnesota, where I live in a kind of financial exile from Manhattan. Interrupted midshine by a cry of distress from Sweet Polly ("Oh where, oh where has my Underdog gone . . . ?"), he humbly, lovably mumbles, "Excuse me, sir, I'll finish the other shoe tomorrow," and trots into a nearby phone booth. It explodes, revealing a rather off-the-rack superhero in a baggy red jumpsuit and a ratty blue cape that regularly tangles him up.

As you'll have guessed, I was a weird kid. Until I turned twelve, I faked a British accent. I wore a tie, even though it wasn't part of the Cranbrook School for Boys' dress code. In the school band, my instrument was the bongo drums. Not only was I an immigrant, born in South Africa, but my parents had been desperately poor as children and had made good—my father was a doctor, my mum a doctorate—and they seemed to think that the children of those who'd done well for themselves dressed up in safari outfits and carried butterfly nets. Their idea of privilege came not from hands-on experience but from reading *Brideshead Revisited*.

I'm still eccentric. I like ballet and Bernese mountain dogs, I overdress for picnics, and often wonder what you're laughing at. The sheep could all zig, and we freaks may be a little lonely, but at least we're different. Eccentrics are heroes to me. At least they have a point of view.

So, yes, I related to Underdog. I don't think my mother made this connection, but I did: he's a dog in a world of humans, an outsider, a nut. He's sweet natured; his motives are good. But there is no sense, no way, he fits in. He has no sidekick, no pals, no family, no club. Like me, he had only his own soul, his spirit, and his superpowers. He's not an outcast exactly, since he's a celebrity. People like him without knowing him. As with so many superheroes, he is forced to live with a terrible secret that strands him from the world he tries to save. There's no better way to describe how I feel: polite, good intentioned, even liked, in a way, but a different species from the rest of you. Maybe everybody feels this way.

Much later, when I met my wife, she and some friends were talking about an episode of *The Brady Bunch,* and somebody asked me what I thought.

"I've never seen it," I said.

"Yeah, right."

"I've never seen *The Partridge Family,* either."

"Impossible."

"But I loved *Underdog.*"

"Hey, me, too!"

I have never run into a fellow Gen Xer who didn't. Not one.

Turns out, you don't need a broad range of references to 1970s syndicated television to be in the swim. You only need one, deeply felt, and an ability to steer the conversation there. I was lucky my mom picked that show and not, say, *Tennessee Tuxedo. Underdog* is a universal connector.

Which doesn't mean the show is perfect, of course. It had some problems with logic that bothered the left side of my brain.

Like: If Underdog blows them up each week, why isn't his town's population of phone booths reduced to zero?

Like: If Sweet Polly Purebred is a purebred, what's her breed? Nobody knows. Believe me, I've asked around. There's a trend toward beagle, a suspicion of Cavalier King Charles spaniel, maybe some Maltese. The fluffy white coat, black button nose, and air of annoying self-obsession make me think she's a handbag-type dog, which I've always despised.

Like: Why is the town's biggest business establishment called the Two-Cent Savings Bank? Who *saves* two cents?

And while we're at it, why is he even called Underdog? Your classic underdog is some schlump with a sack full of sorrows who batters down the locked doors of fate with a combination of faith, pluck, and persistence. (Malcolm Gladwell wrote a book showing he also needs a lot of luck.) Our Underdog—capital "U"—in contrast, is a world-famous superstar with a unique and well-recognized brand. Governments call on this dude. In one episode, when we're threatened by an evil overlord from the Planet Granite, the *Earth itself* has nowhere else to turn.

Rocky Balboa, sure. William "Braveheart" Wallace. Oliver Twist. The 2014 Seattle Seahawks. The 2011 Denver Broncos. Harry Potter. Colonel Sanders. Susan Boyle, indeed. *The Mighty Ducks!* Inspiring underdog stories, every one. But Underdog himself? Not quite.

Then there's the theme song, chanted like a horse opera over images of tanks rolling into town:

> *Speed of lightning, roar of thunder,*
> *fighting all who rob or plunder . . .*

Pause button. There's a lot of villainy in the series, of course, some of the rascaliest in the annals of animation, but most of the nemeses' crimes don't involve anything so trivial as *robbery*.

Underdog's archrival is a weaselly little cube-shaped menace named Simon Bar Sinister, who talks like a hemorrhoid and whose catchphrase is, "Simon says . . . [insert diabolical command here]!" His dreams run to global domination, not plunder. He is your classic control freak. In him, a deep and aching loneliness and fear of never finding love expresses itself—via the alchemy of advanced mental illness and a background in engineering—in a strange way: he builds ray guns. His ray guns do things like turn people into snow, two-dimensional photographs, or turkeys.

Of course, at some level, the show is pure parody. The hero speaks in rhymed couplets: the word is, um, *doggerel*. *Superman* is mocked all over town. Our dog and the humble, lovable Clark Kent share more than tragic glasses, epic shyness, phone booths, capes, flight, superstrength, and a fetish for bitchy journalists. They share a clean-cut earnestness that speaks to all the socially awkward, conflict-averse kids, like me—like everyone I knew—who wanted a lot of attention for doing great things but realized it would take pills or magic or a miracle to get us over the hump.

And there's another rhythm to the show that accounts for its appeal, at least to me. It's this: despite superstrength, the ability to fly, X-ray eyes, and atomic ears—and despite a sick-making talent called "atomic breath," shared by most dogs—despite all this, Underdog is a total disaster.

He's an antisuperhero, or a superzero. Let's say he's what I would be if I actually got superpowers: kind of dangerous, and not in a sexy way. Rather than some himbo in a jumpsuit with the secret sauce, our beagle is a goofy gus who gets banged up on his way to the rainbow. He's what the suits in Hollywood would call relatable.

In the beginning, the show didn't mention Sweet Polly or pep pills, but it had all the essentials. A boy is locked in a bank vault. (We never find out why, or why no one can open it—typical cartoon logic.) Underdog appears and breaks open a vault. Turns out, it's in the wrong bank.

"You harebrained Hercules!" says the manager.

Locating the right vault, Underdog pops it open, but somehow loses the kid.

"What good are you, you crackpot?!" says the man.

Like some demented Rube Goldberg machine, Underdog then uses his X-ray eyes to set the bank on fire, blows it out with his atomic breath—and, miraculously, sitting in a smoldering postapocalyptic landscape, there's the missing kid, holding a balloon.

"Is there some reward we can give you for this mess— uh, job?"

Underdog never takes a reward. Like Spider-Man, he's repaid by good feelings. And the collateral damage he does is outrageous. He doesn't like doors. To exit a building, he simply heads north, smashing through floor after floor. That's one way to beat traffic, I suppose.

Confronted by complainers, his response is always the same:

"I am a hero who never fails.
I can't be bothered with such details."

And yet, we know that he is bothered.
Fade out.

Part 2

What most people remember today are the pills. Ask anyone about Underdog, and they'll say something like "He took a lot of drugs." It's too bad, really. Those pills loom larger in memory than in fact. Underdog was supercanine without the juice. He used it sparingly—when he needed a boost. Unlike Popeye's spinach, Scooby's snacks, or Roger Ramjet's proton pills, Underdog's "super-energy pills," which he kept in a compartment in his ring, mafioso style, were pretty much a supplement.

They showed up in episode 10 and reappeared from time to time, always causing his eyes to splash fireworks and American flags. There's some confusion about whether the pills were supposed to encourage kids to take vitamins or were simply an artifact of a simpler time, when "mother's little helper" was a common crutch. For syndication, references to "super-energy pills" were changed to "super-vitamin pills," and in the 1990s the pills were written out entirely.

Still, there's no denying that at times our hero looks like a stone junkie. There's the episode where he's trapped in a water-filled room with Polly and he loses his ring.

"Without my super-energy pill
I grow weaker and weaker and weaker still."

His eyes get filmy, his mouth parched. He begs Polly to swim around looking for his fix. In another episode, as I remember it, a single pill dropped in the city's water supply gives the entire population the power to smash concrete. This is good stuff.

Oddly, I never did drugs. Another sign of a deprived childhood. I was too uncool to get invited to those parties frankly, and I'm terrified of breaking the law. Also, I've always felt like my grip on sanity was marginal enough not to force it to go anywhere strange. And lest you wonder if I'm going to burst into prayer, let me assure you that I did not escape the net. I am most definitely an alcoholic.

Looking back at *Underdog* now, it's almost uncanny how he nailed the themes of my life. There's the reliance on a chemical to make me better, faster, stronger. Unlike Underdog, I never rescued anyone from anything when I was drinking. The biggest adventures I got into mainly involved passing out and waking up on the other end of the couch. But I turned to my secret sauce for super-powers with girls and later, disastrously, at work.

And then there's dogs. Underdog may be no underdog, but he's very like a dog—warmhearted, excitable, not too smart. As I get older, what I value in myself is the little I have left from the 1970s. I suppose what I mean is a simple sweetness, an ability to love: the qualities I see in Underdog, in any dog.

Pet haters, I ask you: What can you be thinking? Cats aren't to be trusted, of course, but there's nothing suspicious about dogs. Most of them have a boneheaded warmth that I find almost unbearably poignant. My beloved Bernese mountain dog, Hola, was a terrible puppy—as I was a terrible drunk—and the process of trying to train her to pass her Canine Good Citizen certification test from the American Kennel Club was the basis of my recovery from alcoholism. Hola trotted me through the steps. She made me believe in God and in God spelled backward, and I owe her more than I can say. I wrote a book, *Bad Dog (A Love Story)*, about her. Even that is not nearly enough.

Yet Hola is just doing what dogs do. I had a dog when I was a kid. His name was Sammy, and he'd sometimes watch *Underdog* with me. I should explain that Sammy was more than one dog—he was a series of standard poodles brought home from my dad's medical lab in downtown Detroit. My parents kept up a halfhearted pretense that "Sammy" was a single animal, but even my little sister, whose vision was never that hot, picked up on the inconsistencies.

"That's not Sammy," she said one day, over a bowl of King Vitaman.

My mum looked at my dad, and the expression in her puppy eyes seemed to say: *This is too weird even for us.*

Sammy went back to the lab. Dogs often have to live

that way, at the mercy of forces beyond their control. It's
not fashionable, but I think that's true of people, too. It's
true of me. We try so hard with good intentions and end
up getting called back to the lab, leaving nothing behind
but a television playing to an empty room.

So what is Underdog's kryptonite? His fatal flaw? This
is not an easy question to answer, unless you want to say
"himself" (which may be the answer for most of us). I
think it's Sweet Polly. She's the substance that endangers him.

Announcer: "A shoe shine puppy transforms himself
into a superhero every time Sweet Polly Purebred gets
in trouble."

Luckily for us viewers, she's incredibly accident prone.
Our hero carries buildings around, saving us from destruction, when his nemesis, Simon Bar Sinister, decides
to invent a weather machine disguised as a gothic pipe
organ right out of *The Abominable Dr. Phibes.*

"Simon says . . . tornado twist!"

Meanwhile, Sweet Polly is on location at Cape Carnival [sic], covering a Moon launch. In a clear breach of
NASA protocol, Polly is allowed to ride along to the
Moon. Bar Sinister and his sidekick, Cad Lackey, replace the real astronauts, hijack the rocket, and announce their evil intentions.

"I want . . . to take over the world!"

Bar Sinister's demands are always elegantly simple:
"Agree to make me dictator of all Earth!"

Of course, all Earth has nowhere else to turn but . . .

Underdog. His solution is to spin so fast he disappears, zip up to the Moon, start a comical who-did-that/not-me fight between the supervillains, and rescue the dizzy girlfriend he refuses to touch.

You heard me. Recall what happens after Underdog saves the girl from the pincer grip of the ten-story robot monster using his ultrasonic "hi-fi sound" to smash the vacuum tubes in its brain, meanwhile breaking every window, mirror, lightbulb, and pickle jar in town.

A flushed, grateful Polly pushes toward him with a pucker. And what does he do? Backs away, like some preteen goofball.

"True heroes are never paid," he stutters. "And I'm the truest hero ever made."

His is an absolutely innocent love, made more innocent by Wally Cox's tentative talk track. Superman may have fought for truth, justice, and the American way, but Underdog's mission is the more pure. I think he fought like a dog for unconditional love.

And that, my friends, is my kind of superhero.

Now a hideous giant appears terrorizing the city, and the announcer says: "Looks like this is the end!"

SUPERMAN: ONE RAD DUDE

JIM DI BARTOLO

AUTHOR AND ILLUSTRATOR

I want Superman to be real.

I don't want some limited-in-power, morally vague, generally good other hero X or Y. I want the Big Blue Boy Scout and I want him one hundred years ago. Hitler versus Superman? World War II is over in less time than it takes for me to get annoyed when someone says, "But Kryptonite . . . !" To which I say, "*No*, because they'd never get close enough for it to have an effect."

Still reading this? That's how fast Superman would win. (Also, thanks for still reading!)

Of course that's all speculation and opinion, and I'm biased because I think he's awesome. I'm also biased because Superman has helped me on countless days for as long as I can remember, and I'm sure I'm not the only one.

I can't begin to fathom the crushing, powerless frustration that causes victims of war and violence to crave a superhero. Though opinions vary as to what specifically drove Jerry Siegel and Joe Schuster into creating Superman all those years ago, I have little doubt that some of that drive was a result of being the children of Jewish immigrants amid the overseas horrors of World War II. In various situations and life circumstances, most of us can probably relate to their want of a hero in so many ways.

My mother and father always raised me with an awareness of right from wrong, generosity versus self-ishness, Good versus Evil. And though I would briefly sport a mullet in my teen years, I have otherwise tried to live a morally good life. I grew up with phrases like "Don't lie. You'll only have to cover it up with more lies" and "Don't ever bully someone, because if we've raised you right, you'll always regret it" and other lessons still (thankfully) ringing in my ears to this day. So most likely my parents laid the groundwork for me to embrace what Superman stands for. He has loomed large in my life from the long-ago days of the *Super Friends* and my early exposure to comic books, when the filter of "What would Superman do?" began to run through my brain. Indirectly, he offered me an illusion of safety while the world's political turmoil gave me unease. Later, he helped show me what it was to be a man as a sometimes bullied adolescent and teenager. Even now, he lends a handy gauge as I make my way, sometimes with composure and style, and sometimes with pit stains and poorly trimmed nose hair, through adulthood.

I grew up in the United States with oftentimes flawed examples of what "a man is supposed to be," hearing things like "do this—" or "eat this—it'll put hair on your chest." Awesome! Just what seven-year-old-me wanted: a premature pube rug on my pale, bony chest.

It's easy to forget now that children of the 1980s genuinely feared Nuclear Armageddon. On top of which, I was living near an air force base that was considered a major nuclear target during that goofy-fashioned hyperjingoistic Cold War era. The threat of nuclear evaporation was such a staple that we had to do drills at school, practicing how and where to cower in case of a nuclear attack. Even at a very young age I didn't think my flip-top desk offered much lifesaving protection. Perhaps understandably, I sometimes vanished into the daydream escape of Superman being able to save everyone in one fell swoop if nuclear war did indeed begin. I was old enough to know he wasn't real. Still, his "do what is right" character trait seemed powerful enough to offer some real-world comfort when the TV news would terrify me, or when the local newspaper would do something shitty like publish a front-page illustration showing the blast radius of a nuclear bomb hitting Castle Air Force Base—complete with the number of nanoseconds my neighborhood would survive once the bomb hit. Thanks, Teddy from the graphics department—you succeeded in mentally scarring my psyche for decades, you unhinged, newspaper graphics department lunatic.

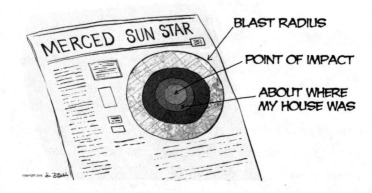

But Superman wouldn't only save us, he would bring the bad guys to justice! Or at the very least, go to their country, Ocean's Eleven all their nuclear bombs, and Hail Mary them into deep space, right?

In comics, when Superman gets involved in politics or with mankind on a larger scale, it's sometimes shown to be a slippery slope. For me, Superman has never been the easily manipulated nitwit portrayed in Frank Miller's *Dark Knight Returns* but rather a man/alien who could evaluate situations and suss out right from wrong without the influence of persuasions or bribes.

The very fact that he restrains himself from full-on face stomping Lex Luthor is either an incredible display of his solid morality—and thank you very much, Jonathan and Martha Kent, for his good manners—or evidence that he just really hates having to scrub disintegrated teeth and pulped brain from his boots. Being an optimist about his character and the job his Earth parents did, I choose the former.

There was also the comfort of relatability—yes, relatability—to Superman (and of course, Clark Kent) when

I would get bullied in grade school. Though never over-whelmingly targeted or dramatically degraded (never pantsed, or even wedgied), still, I was subjected to taunts and physical threats for such offenses as:

1) *being a good student* or
2) *having fair skin* or
3) *having red (ish) hair.*

My response of "carrot tops are green, genius" never seemed to convince anyone to stop calling me that. Sadly, logic is not the best defense on the playground. And, no, no matter how much I have tried, I can only burn, not tan. Yes, frustratingly, Earth's yellow sun gives me no su-perpowers, though it did eventually give me stage 1 mela-noma (i.e., skin cancer) for my youthful efforts of tan *attempting.*

I wasn't even consistently a class suck-up either. I mean, I'm sure we have all done *some* of that, right? And, yeah, I'm going to dismiss the notion that I *might* have

been bullied once or twice because of it. Give an example,
you say? Okay, there was that *one time* in the fifth grade
when Mrs. Trumble asked who among us would bring
an old toothbrush from home for ne'er-do-well Donald
Norbitt to clean the classroom's sink with, and, yes, I
immediately raised my hand. But who are we kidding?
Donald really trashed that sink! Paint and powdered
soap everywhere. We're living in a society here, is what
I'm saying. First the sink, then the whole back counter-
top, and next he's kidnapping politicians' kids for ransom.

You've got to shut it down early is my point.

Ultimately, it was a wise decision (or, through hindsight: fortuitous cowardice) that I never struck out at my
bullies, because while I've since practiced martial arts
for many years, eight-to-twelve-year-old me had the
kinesthetic skill set of a spastic toddler.

But amid whatever taunts I suffered, I could find kinship and strength from Clark when he was bullied for
being bookish (in stories where he was shown in school),
or for being clumsy or a "country bumpkin" when working at the *Daily Planet*. And while now I may or may not
be guilty of some social-media-schadenfreude moments
against those who teased me, I still try my best to rise
above that negativity and be more like Kal-El.

When I reflect on what is sometimes years and years
of less-than-stellar *Superman* comics to see if they
really were as bad as we all thought at the time (yes, they
were!—I should really put those up on craigslist), there
were, however, two near-perfect 1980s *Superman* movies

for young me to cling to. Both offered up reminders of why doing what is right and being a good person are the things to strive for, and I love them for that. No reasonable person would ever ask themselves "What would Lex Luthor or General Zod do?" when their parents asked them to stop picking their nose and go clean their room. And though my ten-year-old self was sometimes confused (in my pants) by my nagging attraction to the wicked Ursa, she and her crew of Zod and Non were simply big-screen adaptations of the bullies I encountered in elementary school. To this day, that school yard bully trait is something I despise in those around me as well as in politicians, celebrities, and athletes.

So despite Ursa making me feel kind of funny (still in my pants) and conflicted, I always knew she needed to be defeated.

Those two films stood out to me especially given the fact that most other movies of that era had their heroic male leads glibly killing off cookie-cutter villains left and right. As long as those deaths were framed by a pun or some form of cold-blooded humor, it was bankable. And while I watched my own fair share of blood-splattered-justice flicks back then, it's no surprise to me that the optimism of the first two *Superman* movies holds up far better than the ammo-and-testosterone-turned-to-eleven movies have.

Nowadays, whether I'm out and about sporting the one-two combo of a Supes T-shirt and my Superman logo tattoo, or at home drawing and painting while periodically searching eBay for cool action figures, I go happily into the sunset of nerddom knowing that while Hollywood might never get him right again—and the comic book industry itself even sometimes falls short on delivering a good long-term Superman story—he'll continue to be one of my main internal sounding boards and a role model for generations to come. And though he's both lovingly and mockingly called "the Big Blue Boy Scout," I'll take that label, thank you very much, and embrace it till I die.

So when people tell me that dark hero X would beat Superman, or that our world is too gritty or pessimistic for such a pure and good hero, I know they're wrong, and I hope they figure that out, too. Because he really can inspire us all to be better, and do better, and to leave the world *at least a little bit* better than how we found it.

And if you disagree, I can probably find my old teacher for all of you needing some of that fifth grade classroom Mrs. Trumble–style justice. Consider yourself warned, because she was seriously intimidating, and I bet eBay and Craigslist have weird shit like old toothbrushes on there.

SOME INTERSTITIAL THOUGHTS ON THE IN-BETWEENER

CHARLES YU

The In-Betweener, is, in essence, the synthesis of everything I like about comics. How comics created my sense of the universe, both real and fictional, and how stories can move in, through, across, outside, and in between fictional worlds. Comics gave me my conceptions of space and time, of reality. Of malleability and fixitude. And the In-Betweener is the purest example of what and why and how comics do that.

More than the actual character itself, I like the idea of the In-Betweener. Which isn't to say I only meta-like him—because in a way, the In-Betweener is exactly the same as the idea of the In-Betweener. With these cosmic entities, that's sort of the point. The reason I like him, though, isn't nearly so high-minded. For me, the great thing about the In-Betweener is what his existence means about the Marvel Universe as a whole.

Let me explain that a little more.

* * *

I was twelve when I first came to terms with the possibility that I might not be a superhero. I wasn't positive, of course, and had every interest in withholding final judgment on the matter until I could be sure. But the possibility was there. I'd been an early bloomer, and that advantage, combined with having an early January birthday, resulted in a stretch during which I was able to enjoy some very unfair athletic success against kids who had not yet had the benefit of puberty. For about eighteen months, I was faster, stronger, and bigger than anyone else in my grade, and there seemed to be no ceiling on my potential right up until I ran smack into the brick wall of reality: other kids. Kids who were, like me, big for their age, and unlike me, actually gifted at sports.

There was even an exact moment when I realized it: back stretch, 400m final, regionals, Arco/Jesse Owens track meet, spring of 1988. I'd made it this far—next stop was the state meet. In the early qualifying meets, I'd jogged to easy wins, and for the first 320 meters or so of this final, I had no reason to believe anything would be different. And then, it all went wrong.

So, so wrong. When the first kid passed me, it was a bit demoralizing, sure. But still nothing to worry about. I might even be able to catch him. But I didn't catch him. Instead, another kid passed me. Uh oh. Huh. Well. Bummer, but top three qualified for state, so I was still okay. Then, just before the finish, a third kid passed me,

leaving me in fourth. No state. No medal. The only
thing I earned that day was the first taste of my non-superhero-ness.

So, okay, twelve years old, and freshly retired Olympic hopeful. Time to take stock of the situation. I was still smart, a good student. Maybe that'd be my key to being extraordinary. I'd have to get a little more creative now, do a little work to define my power.

I wasn't starting from zero. Along with my brother Kelvin, I'd been presiding over a small universe for several years by that point, the most powerful being in existence. (Kelv, being two years younger, having to settle for being number two which, I assured him, was not bad at all, although being his own man, I'm sure he didn't appreciate the consolation prize.) Together, we ruled over the cosmos with wisdom, benevolence, and a wide variety of energy beams that we could shoot from our eyes, fingers, hands, or even brains if necessary.

In the aftermath of the Arco/Jesse Owens regionals, however, there were obviously now elements of this personal narrative that were, even to my twelve-year-old self, no longer tenable. I'd have to come up with a new hook.

Many superheroes are, in some sense, abstractable. Which is not to say they are abstractions themselves—they have backstories and adoptive parents and people they have lost, people who have hurt them, and people whom they hurt. But none of those particularities diminish the central, defining feature of the most powerful heroes: namely, that they have a central, defining feature. This is, in a fundamental, almost definitional sense, what distinguishes a superhero from a non-superhero: no matter how screwed up he or she is, there is at least one feature of awesomeness. The awesomeness is part of their very identity. It's how people know them, it is the source of their power (and often their greatest weakness), it manifests itself in ways big and small. The Flash talks fast. He thinks fast. He has lightning bolts on his temples and ankles. The Flash-ness of the Flash goes all the way down into his core essence, and manifests outward, even to the decorative flourishes on his hero-gear. This generalizability (speed, personified; weather, personified; rage-strength, personified; etc.), combined with rich and detailed backstories, makes these characters both universal and particular.

But above the stratum of top-shelf heroes, way, way out of reach of even the most powerful "regular superheroes," there are entities (at least in the Marvel Universe) that are, in fact, pretty much straight-up personified ideas, incarnations of philosophical concepts. Galactus. The Stranger. The Living Tribunal. For me (and I suspect I'm not alone in this), comics were the first exposure I ever had to metaphysics, to allegory—and probably the deepest and most sustained exposure at that.* When, in the second semester of my senior year in high school, we read *Waiting for Godot* in AP English, my first and most helpful reference for what I was reading were comic books. I recognized Beckett as working in the same genre as Stan Lee and Jack Kirby, or if not exactly the same genre, then at least in an adjacent neighborhood. And as far as I can tell, there's no one more conceptual than the In-Betweener.

According to the Marvel Universe Wiki (www.marvel .com/In-Betweener), "the conceptual beings Lord Chaos and Master Order created the In-Betweener and charged him with the task of keeping the cosmos in balance for them." The In-Betweener has also been described as the synthesis of life and death, order and chaos, love and hate, god and man. Which is, you know, a little heavy. If Hegel ever got to write an issue for Marvel, it's hard to imagine him coming up with a more Hegelian character than the In-Betweener.

Just in case the weirdness of this character is not fully apparent from the foregoing, I would like to restate it in a slightly different manner. The In-Betweener was

---

* Comics are also the first exposure most people ever have to metafiction (retcons, crossover stories, Crises on Infinite Earths, etc.). Bugs Bunny might have been the first fictional character who ever broke the fourth wall for me, but comic books took it to an entirely different level. But that's a topic for a different essay.

created by *Lord Chaos* and *Master Order*. These aren't cute names for arch-nemeses. These are cosmic entities, creating another abstract entity, who is the synthesis of two other abstract entities.

In other words, what I loved and love and will always love about the Marvel Universe is that it is seriously *dense*.

It isn't some sketch, some façade of a cosmos. This is the real thing—a fully-imagined fictional space-time thick with more detail than you anticipated. Definitely more detail than you could come up with yourself. And probably, if we're being honest, more detail than you actually want to know.

Granted, if we're just looking at the raw stats, the In-Betweener is not exactly awe-inspiring—maybe not even fearsome. That's because, even though as a cosmic entity the In-Betweener is technically one of the most powerful beings in the Marvel Universe, based on his actual win-loss record within his weight class he's kind of a punching bag. By my count, his head-to-head battle appears to be either 1–5 or 1–6, depending on whether or not you want to say his battle with Galactus, which Galactus was winning, is a win or a loss for the IB.

Either way, it's not a stellar record, but it's also a reflection of the fact that the In-Betweener only fights other cosmic-level, universal-level entities. He fights in his weight class. He's like a perennial title contender who has the bad luck of fighting the best during his prime—

the In-Betweener is like Larry Holmes to Muhammad Ali. Each loss is, in a way, proof of his greatness, for him to even be in the ring. And these were close losses. To borrow a framework for how to think about the world from Kevin Seccia, understanding the world for a twelve-year-old boy often comes down to one question: in a fight between any two entities, who beats up the other guy?

At one point in his life, maybe during a mid-life crisis, the In-Betweener (who as noted above, was never very happy with his situation, as an inherently self-conflicted abstraction whose very essence was to be in tension with himself) tried to basically quit his job as a flunky for Lord Chaos and Master Order, by cozying up to the Elders of the Universe, hoping to get Galactus's job as an eater of worlds/general cosmic badass.

Unsurprisingly, Galactus was not cool with this, and handed the In-Betweener one of his several defeats at the hands of beings slightly more all-powerful than the nearly all-powerful In-Betweener.

And yet, to a twelve-year-old looking for comfort and/or inspiration, the idea that there might be a place in the world for someone other than the very strongest, or fastest, or most in control of various aspects of the electro-magnetic spectrum, was powerfully alluring. The notion that there could be someone whose particular powers or talents or just quirks, however middling or even minor, might still be worthy of inclusion as canon, might still be notable enough to merit a title, a name, a storyline, however buried. The kinds of characters who only the most obsessive, exhaustive, meticulous, protective, and even possessive fans would know about. And in a place like the Marvel-verse, just where there should be such a character, there is one.

When I was a kid, I thought that when I turned the TV off, the characters' lives stopped. And then I was fascinated by the idea that their lives didn't. Wrong both ways, of course. In the Marvel Universe, they do have lives. Whole lives. Whole mythologies, that are there, whether you like it or not. It gives the feeling of an existence that could care less whether you know about it. The eternal verities. A discovered thing.

Looking at it that way, it's not so weird. The memory of a nine-year-old me, standing in the comic book shop on Overland Avenue in Culver City, California, sifting through titles and covers, flipping through the latest, looking for undercover philosophy, is pretty ridiculous. On the other hand, it's completely natural. Nine, eight, seven, that's plenty old enough to be thinking about creation, about existence, about not just good and evil, but being and non-being. My six-year-old already has her own cosmology developing, and is building it out, piece by piece, with scraps of information that she comes by, from books, from TV, from friends, from me, from her own imagination. Children absorb these bits into their working theories of the world, they ingest and incorporate and digest and revise, and they iterate, working toward the ability to generalize, from their collected impressions, principles, underlying rules and dynamics, to be able to abstract universal ideas. Later in adolescence, or even a few years after that, absolutes break down, boundaries reveal themselves to be porous. But for a few years, late grade school for me, I was an amateur metaphysician, putting together my grand unified theory. Which is to say, for a nerdy weirdo like I was (and am), a story about creation, a foundational origin myth, a cosmology in which I might have some role, however modest. A role like that of the In-Betweener, a nearly omnipotent entity who has, in the long history of the universe, made a grand total of 84 appearances in 59 different titles. A vanishingly small number—and yet, not zero.

Since then, he has not turned up in an issue, but that doesn't mean he is not out there. He exists. In the world. And it gives me pleasure to think of his existence, this lost, hidden character, living in the shadows.

I'm a dad now, with two kids of my own, ages eight and six, and they have long loved stories of all kinds. They already intuitively understand shared universes, crossover episodes, mythology, and backstory. I love creating worlds with them, in their rooms, in our family room, on the couch, in the car, in our heads, love exploring other people's worlds as well. And I know I'm not a superhero—not even close. A lot of days, I feel like maybe

I'm the opposite—a secret villain. Maybe Order and Chaos—except what I'm trying to do is produce a superhero myself.

But that's not the goal, is it? To make them superheroes? Not really, no. It's something less grandiose but, I hope, more crucial for them as cosmic entities. Other than keeping them safe from villains, super and otherwise, my primary goal, as I see it anyway, is to maximize their capacity for wonder. To teach them about the dense universe we live in, an inexhaustible supply of places to hide, to hang out, to discover. To hand down to them, as best as I can, my own crude map of the landscape, a world crammed with stories and stories and stories, with so many nooks and crannies and crevices and hiding places that they could start today and spend every day of their lives looking, and they'll never stop finding new things, hiding there, between the pages.

SUPERHEROES AND TRAUMA

BECOMING BETHANY

A LIFE IN SEVEN DEATHS

ALETHEA KONTIS

"Amazing! I don't know who wrote the training program for you kids, but he did an astonishing job of equipping you for crisis situations."
—*Willis Ducummen*

"Unfortunately, it seems to have given them a rather extreme way of dealing with those crises."
—*Tony Murcheson*

When strange things happen—extreme bad or good luck, a series of synchronicities, exceptionally great timing—people will say "Just like in the movies!" or "I swear, my life is a sitcom." When events begin to border on ridiculous, folks might liken their lives unto the plot of a soap opera. When this business goes from bizarre to ludicrously unbelievable, one might very well be living in a comic book.

For me, 2014 reached comic book proportions . . . and I was Bethany.

Bethany (no last name) was one of the original five of

John Byrne's Next Men. The Next Men was a secret initiative started by the U.S. government in the 1960s, in which babies were raised in a *Matrix*-like computer in an effort to speed up human evolution. Most test subjects failed, but five young people survived with their genes triggered to enhance certain abilities. Danny could run superfast. Nathan could see well beyond the normal human spectrum. Jack had superhuman strength. Bethany was invincible.

It was Jack who inadvertently broke the five out of their utopian, shared dream world (known as the Greenery) and brought them forth into the Real World, where their supertraits began to get decidedly out of hand. Danny's leg muscles grew so large that he could not wear normal pants. Nathan's eyes didn't look human anymore. Jack could barely touch a thing without destroying it. But the price for Bethany's invincibility was probably the highest. She began to feel nothing at all, no cold, no heat. She had no sense of touch or taste. Her hair was sharper than razor blades and her fingernails could punch right through a man's chest. Eventually she lost all pigment in her skin and hair. The numbness spread inside as well, and Bethany became emotionally detached from the other Next Men. They called her Hardbody. Meanwhile, the line between the universe we know and the one we read about in comic books was beginning to blur . . .

I reread the first thirty issues of *JBNM* before writing this essay. What struck me most is how little Bethany actually appears on the page. And yet her story had made such an impression on me when I read the comic back in high school that she was the character that immediately sprang to mind after my maternal grandmother passed away in 2013 and the numbness swept over me.

After six long years of the Alzheimer's downward spiral, Memere's death might have been anticipated, but it was never going to be easy. Memere's passing was the first significant family death I had experienced since I was very young. I got the call the morning of Superbowl Sunday, threw some clothes together, jumped in the car, and drove ten hours from D.C. to Vermont. Memere was long past the stage of coherency, but my mother and big sister and I all managed to be there to hold her hands as she died. I heard later that the lights went out in the Superdome that night. A fitting coincidence.

Needless to say, I was not okay for a very long time. But like all experiences, I learned a lot. About the world. About myself. About what I could handle, physically and mentally. The year after Memere's death was my training ground, my Greenery; and in that place I prepared myself for anything and everything life could throw at me. And then the machines of the universe slipped a cog.

Ah, hubris.

The First Death: Experience

In January, eleven months after Memere passed away, we learned that my boyfriend's grandmother was in the hospital. Granny was a sweet lady—I'd gotten to know her at various family gatherings over the years. She had been hospitalized with pneumonia before. Each time we had come running, and each time she was fine, but still, we never knew.

My boyfriend hadn't exactly been around—in any capacity—for Memere's death, but I never would have done the same to him. Like Bethany, the Greenery had prepared me for what was needed. I cooked meals, played taxi driver, and generally stayed out of the family's way . . . all while attending a local convention at which I'd been scheduled as a guest months before. I painted my face, put on my costume, and warned the organizers that I might have to leave at any moment. As any comic book superhero might.

They told me I was strong. Maybe I was. Not quite Bethany-level numb and invincible, but my "training" held up. I handled the situation as if I'd done it a million times before.

The call came Sunday, right before my last panel. I showed up at the hospital in full regalia, glitter and tiara and the whole nine yards. Granny held on for a couple of days after that. I washed off the glitter, wore the black dress, wept, kissed relatives I didn't know, and went home.

The Second Death: Execution

I was in Philadelphia on Superbowl Sunday, visiting friends and guest judging at a high school debate tournament. I left that morning after checking a few social media updates on my phone and noticing that something seemed to be wrong with a dear friend's three-year-old son. I hoped everything was okay, and then got in the car and drove home. When I arrived, I checked up on her. Everything was not okay. Her newly adopted son, whose Christmas photos were still on my refrigerator, was dead.

That day I learned the difference between an expected death and an unexpected one, between the ending of a mature life and one that never had the chance to blossom. And this was the true anniversary of Memere's passing. So yeah . . . I pretty much lost it. No numbness there.

Not long after, I had a fight with that aforementioned boyfriend. He said some horrible and unforgivable things . . . but nothing he hadn't said before, really. Only this time he raised his hand to me. He didn't hit me, but when he ordered me to leave, I called my mother and booked a one-way ticket to Florida.

After so much sadness, it seems, some numbness does settle in. Bethany's invisible cloak of invincibility settled down around my shoulders as if it had never left. My life had exploded into chaos—much as Bethany's had when the rowdy biker gang tried to beat her and burn her alive. Like her I marched through the flames untouched, one foot in front of the other, believing in my heart that I still fought the good fight.

I spent the next few months of 2014 busy with packing up my worldly possessions and all the figuring out what the heck to do with my-life. I had nightmares of being chased. Of being lost. Of my parents dying. I came out of that last one sobbing the relief of a woman who has wished it was all a dream . . . and then woken to find it *was*.

I went back to D.C. for a month of already-booked appearances and returned to Florida in May with a car-load of stuff, just in time to fly to New York twice for more conferences. The first was the Rochester Teen Book Festival, during which I debuted my new oxblood gown on the red carpet, spinning before the cheering crowd like Katniss Everdeen. The second was Book Expo America, which I finished up with no voice to speak of and tendinitis in both arms.

The next morning, Jay Lake died.

A dear friend and fellow author in the SF genre, Jay had had colon cancer almost as long as I'd known him, almost as long as Memere had had Alzheimer's. Like Memere, we always knew this horrible day was coming, and we all knew it was going to suck. When I discovered the news early that morning, I started crying and couldn't stop. I cried so hard that I could barely see. I wanted to do something for Jay, but I couldn't. Not a eulogy or a farewell . . . I physically could not "say goodbye" without breaking down. I had little over a day before my reading performance at Lady Jane's Salon in which to gather myself. I wore the oxblood dress and lifted a glass in salute to Jay before my reading. It was all I could manage. But I did it, just as I had performed the reading at Memere's funeral.

I had been unable to give that eulogy, too.

I was glad that I'd been with friends when I found out about Jay, but once that day was done, I wanted nothing more than to go home—even if I still had to think a moment about where my home was now—and immerse myself in a cocoon of sensory deprivation. I understood why Bethany pulled away from the people she loved, as comfortable in isolation as Superman in his Fortress of Solitude. Even when a body is perfectly numb, there is still something on the inside, something small and strange and sick. I worried that it was my soul, shrinking away to nothing, and I wanted to hold on to it for as long as I could.

No matter how strong we are, were, or have become, some things are just beyond us. We would like to think we are capable, but those of us who know ourselves also know our own limits. Because we have tested them.

Or so we think.

The Fourth Death: Becoming Bethany

Labor Day. Dragon Con. Atlanta, GA. My yearly pilgrimage to the Land of the Geek, my family reunion of browncoats and caped crusaders. The best part? No overbearing boyfriend. It was the first year in a very long time that I wasn't burdened by the needs of someone else. I was free to stretch myself as far as I could go, to revel in my own beauty and strength. It was exhilarating. Intoxicating. For the first time in a very long time, I was *happy*. I felt like I was floating three inches above the ground the whole time I was there. If I wanted to, I could have flown.

And then this text: Call Mom on your cell when you can.

After that nightmare when I first got to Florida, all I could think was that something had happened to Dad. Isn't that the way with most superheroes?

I had fifteen minutes between panels and the lobby was filled with fans waiting in line, so I ducked behind a column to make the call.

"Are you by yourself right now?" asked Mom.

In a convention of eighty thousand people? Not bloody likely. And yet . . . "It's okay, Mom. Just tell me."

Long pause. Then, "Josh is dead."

Josh.

Not Dad. JOSH.

Josh, my lively, prankster, twenty-five-year-old nephew, the spitting image of Seth Rogen. Dead. Not in a fiery car crash or barroom brawl, as one might have expected, but in his sleep. He'd gone to bed the night before and hadn't woken up the next morning. That was it.

And there I was, with my phone in my hand, behind a column in the lobby of the Westin. My brain raced a million miles an hour, trying to figure out what I needed to do and how I needed to do it. Mom ordered me to stay at the con until the next morning. I still had a full day scheduled, so the timing worked out, but . . . where was I emotionally? Who was I? Could I do this?

I honestly didn't know.

On the other side of that pillar were two old friends. I let them know what had happened. They escorted me into the room and all the way backstage to keep an eye on me.

"You don't have to do this," they said, handing me tissues to catch the tears that would not stop coming.

"I know," I told them. "But I have to try."

"We'll sit in the front row," they said. "If you need to leave at any time, just give us the signal. You can walk out in the middle of the panel. No one would blame you."

I nodded, but I knew I had reached the point of no return. Once I got on that stage, there was no getting off. I would either hold it together or lose it. And I still couldn't stop crying.

I cried right up until I walked through that curtain. And then . . . I became something else. Someone else. I was still *me*, in my body, doing and saying the spectacular and silly things that only I can say or do. I was drawing on some energy deep inside me that I never knew I had . . . or that I hadn't accessed in so long that I'd forgotten it was there. I had transformed. I had evolved.

I had become Bethany.

Bethany, who jumps in front of bullets to protect friends, even if they have betrayed her. Bethany, who faces every foe, no matter how hulking or fierce or armed, because she knows they can't hurt her. Bethany, who may be invincible but still takes her jacket off before she throws a punch. *That* is who I was now. Hardbody.

And I was amazing.

It's a funny thing, strength. People call you strong, when all you've really had the strength to do was keep breathing and putting one foot in front of the other. I had woken up every morning since leaving D.C. feeling like a failure and wondering who the stranger in the mirror was. Who gets admired for that?

So much of courage and strength is about perception. I had been strong and sad, strong and numb, strong and angry, but when I walked out onto that stage at Dragon Con, I was strong and nothing else, inside and out. I was Bethany, immortal and everlasting and nothing could bring me down.

I thought the feeling might leave me as soon as the panel was over, but it didn't. I was in command. I assembled the fan troops and delegated convention tasks. I contacted guest services and let them know the deal. I coordinated with the hotel staff and arranged to leave first thing in the morning. I met with friends and hugged farewells. I barely slept at all, creeping out of the hotel like a thief in the night sometime before five in the morning. I cried and screamed and cried some more, all the way from Atlanta back to Florida.

Mom met me at the door. "Your eyes look worse than mine." And then she hugged me for a very long time.

The toughest thing about my newfound strength was keeping it at bay. I was ready to jump in the car once again and drive the fifteen hours to Vermont, but Mom convinced me to wait and fly with her. I spent the next two days like a caged tiger, like Bethany in a cell.

I puttered impatiently. I unpacked and repacked. I scanned in every photo of Josh I could find to include in the funeral montage. I printed iron-on transfers with Josh's picture on them for the family to wear to the post-funeral reception. I found out that my favorite band would be playing virtually down the street from the reception and I bought two tickets, even if I didn't end up being able to go.

Most important, I decided to give Josh's eulogy.

I didn't know what I was thinking. I didn't even know what I was feeling. But I knew I had one shot, one moment, and if I missed it, it would be gone forever. And yet, this wasn't part of my Greenery training. I hadn't been able to hold it together enough to do this for Memere . . . what on earth made me think I could do it for Josh? My father thought I had gone a little insane. He began to watch me like a hawk.

But he didn't know that I was Bethany now.

Like most children raised Catholic, Josh had respect for religion . . . but he had more respect for life. He was a gadabout and a risk taker. He was passionate and quick to fly off the handle. He liked fast cars and music and drinking and girls. Josh was far more irreverent than he was pious. I was supposed to let some priest who barely knew him give some generic sermon full of lies on his behalf? No way, no how.

I shared the eulogy with no one before the funeral. I typed it up and kept going over it in my head, crossing out words on the plane, waking up in the middle of the night to make edits by the light of my phone. The day of the service, I dressed as Hardbody would, putting on my black corset, tiara, and glitter as if I were going into battle. The priest approached me before the service and informed me that the Catholic Church mandated a time limit on all eulogies. As if I needed more pressure.

I narrowed my eyes at the priest and nodded. He could take that time limit and suck it. *I* wasn't Catholic. I was something better. I was Bethany.

I clung to my ridiculously huge box of tissues and sat myself at the end of a pew, so that I had quick access to the aisle. When the priest waved me over, I took the long walk to the podium, tested the microphone, apologized to Jesus, and then cussed in church. (The title of my essay, "Dammit, Josh!" became a catchphrase that my family still uses to this day.)

I made the assembly cry that day, for that is what happens at funerals, but I also made them laugh, which I will always consider a triumph. I, personally, neither laughed nor cried. I performed my speech perfectly, no tissues needed. I met no one's eyes as I returned to my pew. Nor did I cry through the rest of the service. Instead, I looked at Josh's urn and tried not to burst out laughing because the whole situation was so ridiculous.

I had become Bethany. And, god, was I a mess.

The Fifth Death: Using Your Power for Good

I was still in Vermont when Eugie Foster died. Cancer again. She hadn't even been diagnosed that long ago. I had been spoiled by all those vibrant years we'd had with Jay.

Eugie was a writer of distinction—one day I hope my folktale retelling comes close to the quality of hers. We had met online in a fledgling writers community and gotten to know each other through Dragon Con—for years she headed up the newsletter there. Frail as she was, Eugie had even come to Dragon Con that year. I had stopped in to the Daily Dragon offices, where she usually held court, and found I had missed her by mere moments. I might have tracked her back to her hotel room, shown her my latest costume, and regaled her with my latest exploits, but I knew she was in ill health and did not want to bother her. I never saw her again.

I did not tell my sister about Eugie. My sister was slowly moving forward in the wake of Josh—some good days, more bad days—and I didn't want to derail her progress. Moreover, I felt that I didn't have a right to be sadder than a woman who had just lost her son.

So I mourned in secret. I checked in periodically with my friends online, and I honored Eugie in my own personal way. We had taken my sister for a hike up to Moss Glen Falls that afternoon, a sanctuary of scenic nature painted with fall colors.

A *literal* Greenery.

I released wildflowers into the river and said Eugie's name three times into the sunset as I threw pebbles into the waterfall. On the way back down, my sister asked, "Are you okay?" An oft-repeated question with no good answer. Because when the lines of the world begin to blur, monsters of Herculean proportions pop out of the ether . . . monsters big and strong enough to knock even Bethany to her knees.

"No," I said calmly. "My friend died today."

"Oh," she said. And we continued down the mountain together.

The Sixth Death: Decision

Jesus Gonzales died the day I went to Disney World.

Another writer of distinction, another kind and generous heart, another friend lost to cancer in the blink of an eye. The Disney trip had been on the calendar for months—I had only returned to Florida from Vermont a few weeks earlier. I was to spend a day at the park with a dear friend and her two daughters. We had all been looking forward to this forever . . . and then I woke up to this news, on top of my already unhealthy bank account.

But what kind of horrible person disappoints children? I couldn't. Somehow, I had to find the makeup and cover

up the metaphorical spots on my skin where the color
was fading and pretend that nothing was wrong. Just
like Bethany.

I did not cry when I found out about Jesus, nor as I
spent the morning sending out texts of condolences to
friends who knew him better than I. No, I cried when
my friend paid for my ticket to Disney World.

It seemed that I was now feeling the repercussions of
my superpowers, just as Bethany had. Instead of crying
at sad things, I now cried at kindness. (As of the writing
of this essay, I still do.) I no longer felt emotions as dic-
tated by society, as if I were some denizen of a topsy-
turvy parallel universe. My heart didn't even hurt anymore.
I began to wonder if there was a heart left there at all.

And then I made a decision.

In a side story beyond the core thirty issues of *JBNM*,
Bethany is given the opportunity to go back in time and
change all the bad things that happened to the Next
Men. I'm actually glad my looking-glass world transfor-
mation didn't extend to these particular powers, because
I suspect I might have tried to do the same. I would
have gone back and undone all the death and sadness,
manually flapping those butterfly wings and changing
all the small miracles that were also set in motion by the
universe. Miracles that saved my life.

I had to let go of all the guilt that had been holding
me down. None of these people I loved—*none of them*—
would have wanted me to stop living my life. I was not
dead. Scores of my family and friends were not dead. To

drown myself in sorrow, as tempting as it might have been, would have dishonored their memories. So I decided to live my life to the best of my abilities, and I went to Disney World.

While I was at Disney, I found out my ex-boyfriend's apartment building had caught fire (the ex was fine). Had I not been pushed to leave that toxic environment months earlier, I would have still been there, forced to evacuate my home with a person who loathed me. All this horribleness might have still happened, only I wouldn't have had the immediate support of my parents. Of my extended family. Of my many friends. I would have been set adrift in a lonely world. It does make one pause and wonder about the balance of the universe.

I've read the comics. I know what happens down those dark and twisty roads.

That is how supervillains are made.

The Seventh Death: Becoming Alethea

Fred Grimm had a stroke on Christmas night.

Fred and his wife were convention buddies of mine from Nashville. We went out for Persian food together. We attended local conferences that were boring enough to leave after five minutes and ended up staying far longer because we made our own fun. Fred was one of those people who always left amusing comments on my Facebook posts. Not the ones people make where they try to be funny and fail miserably . . . Fred actually *was* funny. He'd always had the wit and timing of a comic genius.

Given the timing during the holidays, I was not able to drive to Nashville to attend his service, as much as I wanted to. But I stood vigil with his wife, texting love to her and a mutual friend while they sat by his side in the hospital. I shared my favorite pictures and stories of Fred on the Internet. I waited for Fred to recover. We all waited. But Fred did not recover.

After a full weekend of no significant brain activity, we let him go.

But unlike all the other horrible deaths this year, Fred was allowed to live on. Having made his wishes previously known to his wife, Fred was able to donate what organs he could to save other lives. I don't know how many. But I believe in a balanced universe, so I'd like to think at least as many as I lost in twelve months.

That, my friends, is the definition of a true superhero.

I lit a candle and dedicated that week's fairy-tale rant in Fred's honor. I laughed and cried and was proud and cried and hugged my parents and cried and screamed and blew kisses to the Moon and then laughed again. I had cycled back around from numbness to feeling *everything*, every single feeling that was to be felt, sometimes one at a time and sometimes all at once. (I'm even crying as I write this paragraph right now.) And I allowed myself to be that mess. In fact, I was proud of it. For in this last crucible, I realized: I had transcended Bethany.

I have become Alethea.

Whatever I do from here is up to me.

SWASHBUCKLE MY HEART

AN ODE TO NIGHTCRAWLER

JENN REESE

> "Open your heart, Herr Logan. Would it hurt so much
> to see the world through different eyes?"
> —*Kurt Wagner, aka Nightcrawler, to Wolverine*

High school was, among other things, the era of world-ending crushes. I enjoyed my fair share of wistful sighs and classroom daydreams, but instead of writing their names on the pages of my notebook bedecked with hearts and flowers, I wrote their initials on a slip of paper and tucked it under my pillow each night. They were secret crushes, and this magic paper was part wish, part talisman. I knew it was ridiculous even as I was doing it, and yet I did it anyway.

(Note: If you're trying this at home, remember to use *initials only* for maximum deniability. This is especially important if you have brothers.)

Some of the initials I wrote were the same ones everyone was writing in the eighties: HS for Han Solo and IJ for Indiana Jones (two completely different people), SB for Starbuck (classic edition), JC for Jake Cutter, star of the short-lived TV show *Tales of the Gold Monkey*. Rogues, every one! Snide and slick but with a deep moral core that always won through when it was most needed.

But the initials I wrote most often were KW. They didn't belong to a Hollywood hunk like Harrison Ford or Dirk Benedict, or to some emotionally distant Vulcan just waiting for the one girl in all the world who could make him feel. (For the record, I was *totally* that girl.) The initials belonged to Kurt Wagner, a member of the Marvel superhero team the X-Men. His codename was Nightcrawler. (Famous X-Men of this era included: Wolverine, Storm, Cyclops, Jean Grey/Phoenix/Dark Phoenix, Colossus, and the inestimable Kitty Pryde.)

Nightcrawler is a mutant covered in short blue fur. His eyes glow. He has two toes, three fingers, and fangs. He has a tail. He's incredibly agile, especially considering his lack of digits. Mostly, though, he's known for his ability to teleport—to pop from one location to another instantly in a puff of black smoke and brimstone, accompanied by the smell of sulfur and the iconic sound Nightcrawler would become known for (if a sound can be iconic): *BAMF!*

Say it out loud a few times. Picture Nightcrawler in front of you, smiling with those gleaming white fangs against the deep blue of his face. That smile he can make either handsome or wicked, depending on his mood. (He usually chooses both.) And then, *BAMF*. Sulfur, smoke. *BAMF.* You spin and Nightcrawler is behind you, grinning with faux innocence after taping a "Kiss me, I'm a mutant" sign to your back.

Over the years, Nightcrawler's *BAMF* has become the gold standard in teleportation. You want to get from one place to another in the space of a heartbeat, then bamfing is the way the go.

BAMF!

I had an excellent, comfortable middle-class childhood, complicated only by the fact that my father drank too much and was emotionally abusive and prone to random outbursts of rage and violence. A background noise of dread permeated every minute of every day when my father was in the house.

Around other people, my father was universally liked. He was funny and smart, generous to everyone, and quick with a joke in every situation. His secret identity was brilliantly cunning: who would ever believe that this charming, gregarious man was secretly hitting his family and spewing an unending stream of hateful words at them? So we never told. Not teachers or relatives or neighbors or friends. No one would have believed us.

Living isolated and in constant fear warped me. Twisted me. Turned me into something other than what I wanted to be. In comic books, someone might fall into a vat of radioactive waste and emerge a villain. I felt as if I'd fallen into the vat and soaked in it for years.

BAMF!

My first-ever piece of fan art: Nightcrawler falling through space in agony—*AIYEE!*

BAMF!

Kurt Wagner grew up in Germany, abandoned as a baby and later chased by angry townsfolk wielding pitchforks. He couldn't hide what he was; it was writ large in every blue bit of fur on his body, in every swish of his glorious prehensile tail. He looked like a demon, and most regular people thought he'd come from hell. (That's what Nightcrawler's creator, Dave Cockrum, had originally imagined as Kurt's origin story, and Nightcrawler's appearance never changed even when his backstory did.)

Despite growing up hated and feared, Kurt found work as a circus performer and made a family for himself. Later, when Professor Charles Xavier asked him to join the X-Men, he made another family. Everyone liked him: Professor X, his teammates, numerous attractive women. For many years (and countless issues), Nightcrawler was easily the happiest, most well-adjusted member of the angst-filled characters in *Uncanny X-Men*.

He'd been born in that proverbial vat of radioactive waste, but had somehow emerged from it unscathed.

At my house, eating dinner was like entering the X-Men's Danger Room, but with far higher stakes. You survived in one of three ways: by staying perfectly quiet and still, like an innocuous plant or a character from *Jurassic Park* trying to hide from a T. rex; by hoping one of your brothers did something worthy of ridicule and would therefore be receiving the lion's share of the evening's emotional abuse; or by going on the attack. Going on the attack meant pointing out someone else's failings or mistakes in an effort to proactively draw a target on them. Did my younger brother forget a chore? *Use it.* Did my older brother get a C on a test? *Laugh at him.* Did one of them get dumped by their girlfriend? *Gold mine.*

I tell myself this was self-defense. My therapist tells me that, too. I don't believe either of us. Back then, I had two modes: be invisible or be the most dangerous thing in the room.

BAMF!

My second piece of fan art: a copy of the comic book panel featuring a stuffed BAMF doll—a miniature toy version of Nightcrawler himself—seen in the possession of Kurt's girlfriend, Amanda Sefton. Later in the comics, the BAMFs would become a major part of Nightcrawler's story line, but I liked them better when there was just the one, small doll. I used to wonder if it was

Kurt or Amanda who had sewn that adorable little stuffed Nightcrawler by hand, reveling in (rather than reviling) Kurt's furry blue self.

BAMF!

Kurt Wagner idolized Errol Flynn. Kurt was a swashbuckler at heart, daring and extravagant, given to showing off and making quips and coming to the rescue with an excess of panache. A lot of Hollywood swashbucklers fought with a sword in each hand, but Nightcrawler had an advantage. He had a prehensile tail and could fight with three. My heart never had a chance.

BAMF!

I made friends in high school. My first *real* friends. They lent me comics by the box and watched me devour hundreds of issues at a time. It was the comic version of marathoning TV shows on Netflix: you don't nibble on a world, you dive in. Submerge yourself completely. Give yourself over to it.

One of my childhood chores was doing laundry for the whole family. There were five of us, and the mountain of clothes in the small laundry room was perfect for hiding behind with a stack of comics. I'd read one issue and pick up the next without thinking, eager to live in that other world as long as possible before my recalcitrance was discovered. Even when I got caught—and

I always did—I mumbled my excuses and apologies without a modicum of sincerity, no matter how bad the punishment.

How could I be truly sorry when I was living in a world of heroic mutants and supervillains, of created families and swashbuckling romance?

BAMF!

My third piece of fan art: a faithfully redrawn panel wherein Kurt Wagner, aka Nightcrawler, is kissing his girlfriend, Amanda Sefton.

(Please remember that this was the age when VCRs were only just making their way into homes, an age before instant streaming and the World Wide Web. One could only read *Clan of the Cave Bear* so many times.)

Things I will take to my grave: the number of hours I spent staring at this one panel.

BAMF!

In high school, I felt like a mutant fighting against her own genetics. Hurtful things came out of my mouth all the time. *The best defense is a good offense* is a phrase we should apply to war and sports, but not friendships. I think, inside, I was always at war. That background noise of dread kept me perpetually on alert, always ready for a fight. Always ready to start one. I adored Nightcrawler, but I wasn't much like him. No, I was Wolverine. Gruff and quick to push out my claws, a master at hurting the people closest to me. I had incredibly high standards, and I held everyone to them, especially myself. Fall even a little, and *snikt*.

Wolverine was popular in the comics, even back then. I never liked him, and I didn't like myself.

In the real world, demons almost never look like demons. I saw almost daily evidence of this in my father, certainly, but also, with increasing frequency, in the mirror. I was a straight-A student. I had friends. I had plans. I could be funny and gregarious, but I often lashed out and used my wit to slice deep. I was turning into my father.

It wasn't like the comics at all. There was no moment, no spider bite or lightning strike or onset of puberty to turn me from one thing into another. It was a long series of tiny battles fought and lost every day.

BAMF!

For a time, Kurt Wagner had an image inducer that let him hide his demonic visage and masquerade as a human. It was meant to help him blend into a crowd, to pass unnoticed among the nonmutants.

He almost never used it—Kurt was fine with his demon body—but when he did, he usually made himself look like Errol Flynn.

I don't remember individual comic book issues. I can't tell you what my favorite Nightcrawler story line is or when he first met his best X-Man friend, Kitty Pryde. And, thankfully, I stopped reading comics long before the unthinkable happened—before the powers that be decided that Kurt Wagner had to die. (I've since started reading comics again, but I won't go near those issues or that story. He's back again anyway, returned from heaven somehow. This is comics, after all.)

I don't have an encyclopedic knowledge of Kurt Wagner, and honestly I'm fine with that. What I have is an overall sense of lightness. Of humor even in the darkest times. Of swashbuckling fun and friendship, and of a life lived with kindness and passion.

Despite his appearance, Kurt Wagner never had any trouble getting a date. His confidence and swagger overcame any objection to blue fur, and knowing Kurt, he put that prehensile tail to excellent use in the bedroom.

But more than that, Kurt knew how to love. And he always, always felt worthy of love in return.

BAMF!

Recently, a friend (aka my therapist) asked me where I got my strong moral and ethical sense, given that I didn't have any role models for such things while I was growing up. It was one of those crossroads questions where you see all your possible answers stretching out in different directions before you. She knew I was a writer, so I chose the safest answer: "From books. From the heroes I read about." She nodded wisely, pleased, as if she had helped me see a great truth.

I wonder if her expression would have been the same if I'd told her about furry blue Kurt Wagner, about his fangs and his tail and his sulfur cologne. I wonder if I'd still be in therapy.

BAMF!

Here's the thing about slowly turning into a villain, about looking in the mirror every day and seeing a tiny bit less of myself and more of my father: I knew it was happening. Sometimes I knew afterward, when I was beating myself up for all the emotional carnage I'd caused, but sometimes I was self-aware enough to realize what was happening in the moment. Not that I could stop it necessarily. But I would watch my claws come out, could see them going for someone's jugular, and was fully aware of the pain I was causing.

It sickened me. It kept me awake at night. It made me hate myself. And at some point in high school, I'd had enough.

I'd love to say that Nightcrawler alone saved me: that I read one special issue, saw the error of my ways, and became a better person overnight. That's how it works in the comic books—one great catharsis and everyone is rain-

JENN REESE

bows and puppies in the last panel. But recovering is a slow process, and it requires a lot of work.

What Nightcrawler did for me was lead by example. He showed that it was possible to overcome a rough start. That it was possible to find joy amid adversity. That when your own family failed you, you could make your own. He didn't wallow in self-pity and self-hate like Wolverine . . . or like me. He took himself for what he was, and he *reveled* in it. Kurt Wagner took a life born of lemons and spent his years juggling them for laughs.

BAMF!

I made some progress in high school. I won a few battles, lost a few more. But then something glorious happened: I left home for college. Away from my father's oppressive stronghold, I was able to become more of the person I wanted to be. I won more and more battles. Like in comic books, the war never ends. But at this point in my life, I can confidently say that the victory is mine.

BAMF!

Later on in the comics, the writers decided to emphasize Kurt's religious beliefs. He was Catholic, and they turned him into a priest. I'm glad I never read any of those issues. To me, Kurt's religion will always be swashbuckling. It will always be a brilliant smile glowing in the darkness.

BAMF!

I don't put scraps of paper with initials or names under my pillow anymore. (A shame, really, since "Starbuck" works again.) These days, my talismans take different forms: earrings shaped like Captain America's shield. A necklace with Hawkeye's arrow. Three different T-shirts featuring variants of Nightcrawler's grinning face. I'm more Kurt than Logan now—more the fun-loving swashbuckler who, for the most part, has left the past and her demons firmly where they belong. But, hey, we can't all be superheroes. I'll take all the extra help I can get.

In one of the more recent Nightcrawler-centric comics that I've read, good ol' Kurt says, "Raise the flag, X-Men. And let's go be *amazing*."

BAMF!

THE HERO I NEEDED

LIESA MIGNOGNA

If you're from Gotham City, you've heard my story before.

Batman was there for me when no one else was.

When I was small and scared and felt so utterly alone. When just the notion that someone *could* protect me offered protection in itself. When all I needed, more than anything, was simply to be the one who needed.

Most children start out believing in superheroes—in the reassuring presence of all-knowing, all-powerful adults who will always be there and always keep them safe. Who will tuck them in at night and wake them in the morning.

But any fan of superhero stories knows there's a thin line between a hero and a villain, between those who use their gift to help others and those who use it only to help themselves.

My parents divorced when I was eleven months old, and shortly thereafter my father moved several states away. He became a shadowy outline in my world, a man who materialized once a year for a brief visit, then disappeared again. He remained a mystery to me on almost every level—a five-foot three-inch, balding, legally blind, myopically self-centered man with one leg (following a childhood car accident) and one true love—music—who used his talent for piano playing to seduce a string of young, beautiful women into pledging their lives to him, for a series of marriages that didn't end well.

It's my father who made me believe in supervillains. My mother—his third wife, convinced she'd be the one to save him, to change him, to help him become the hero—ended up referring to him as the Sperm Donor. She wised up, and I learned from her mistake—I had to be strong where other women had been weak, I had to resist the urge to fall for a villain.

But as much as I felt his absence in my life as a palpable, aching presence, it wasn't the Sperm Donor who stalked my hometown. The most compelling and dangerous villains in life and literature aren't so terribly obvious—it's the ones who might try to do good, before fate deals them one too many blows. The ones who continue to believe, even in their darkest moments, that their motives are pure—that any destruction they cause to the ones they genuinely love is unavoidable.

I was twelve years old when Tim Burton's *Batman* was released in theaters. The music was haunting and beautiful, the atmosphere of Batman's city—Gotham—breathtaking and chilling. I sat spellbound in the dark and watched for the very first time as young Bruce

Wayne's parents were murdered right in front of him. I saw the loneliness in his eyes as he grew older, the pain and loss and fury that tied him forever to the child he once was.

I saw Bruce channel this into the Batman. I was fascinated, charmed, entranced. Who was this man, larger than life, whispering in and out of the room? Who had an uncanny ability to be there, not always, but just when it mattered most? Who protected and sheltered others, never revealing the sacrifices he made? Who could hold his own against the perfect villain, someone unpredictable, unstable, uncontrollable, and all-consuming?

At the time, I was living in a one-bedroom apartment with my mother. We were supported by welfare while she attended graduate school, studying to be a social worker after being forced to give up her career as a concert flutist due to the degenerative disk disease slowly but surely eating away at her spine.

Welfare checks, food stamps . . . they were laughable means of support. I knew this, because she told me.

She told me everything.

"I'm exhausted," she declared one evening. "I went downtown today to sell my plasma. There's no other way to keep food on the table—how do they expect me to feed my daughter on a hundred dollars of food stamps a month?"

I shook my head, showing her my disbelief—at the

government's stinginess, at her incredible sacrifice, always doing everything she could for me. She sighed. "I had a feeling I wouldn't weigh enough. They check, you know. But I was smart, I put rocks in my pockets before I got there, so they let me through." A wide, slightly maniacal grin spread across her face.

I smiled, too, because she did. I smiled at her cleverness, at this game I recognized—her and me, against the world.

"Sometimes I don't know how I do it. If they hadn't taken my blood today . . . good thing I'm as brilliant as I am funny, right?" She burst out laughing, and I laughed, too. Even in the most serious moments, my mother was always a joker.

A few weeks later, the book I was reading fell right from my hands—it sounded like someone was laughing hysterically in the living room. I ran out and found my mother lying on the floor, pounding her fists into the carpet. It wasn't laughter—she was sobbing, furiously. "I just want to *die*," she moaned. "I can't take it anymore, Liesa." She gulped in more air and then went on, her voice high-pitched and shrill. "I just keep working so hard to make things better. And then there's another bill I can't pay, and the pain is so bad. Nothing ever gets any easier. And we've got this eviction notice, and I don't know what to do. . . . We could be on the street, Liesa, any day now. I just don't see the point anymore. I'm so tired of fighting all the time. It's killing me, trying to keep us afloat on my own." She stopped, giving back over to the sobs, her whole body wracked with them as she pummeled the floor.

Tears sprang to my own eyes and I stood over her, terrified and helpless. My mind raced. . . . I wanted so badly to help her, to save her from all her pain and struggling. But I was afraid, above all else, to lose her and be left completely alone.

"It'll be okay," I finally said. My voice was shaky. I cleared my throat, and tried again, more firmly. "Mom, please, don't say that." I kneeled down next to her, part of me wanting to reach out and touch her—comfort her—but another part deeply repulsed by the sight and sound of her sobs.

My mother's emotions . . . they were always so *big*. They eclipsed everything else, threatened to swallow anyone within reach.

"Mom, we'll figure something out," I pleaded, still unable to get any closer.

Something seemed to penetrate, finally, and the sobs quieted. She sat up and looked at me. Really looked at me.

"Liesa, I'm so sorry," she begged. "I didn't mean it, you know that, right? I would never . . . it's just, I get so overwhelmed sometimes. I'm sorry, baby, I'm sorry."

I began a routine of nighttime suicide checks. When I woke up late, I'd lie in bed frozen, wondering . . . was she still out there? Finally, I would creep out to the living room where she was sleeping, just to make sure.

There were no monsters under my bed or in my closet. Like Bruce Wayne, what scared me wasn't what waited for me in the darkness, but what could slip away.

My mother was as prone to highs as she was to lows. July fourth, every year, we'd head downtown to Baltimore's inner harbor for dinner, and to watch the fireworks. Midway through the meal, my mother would pull out her piccolo. "Everyone loves when I do this," she assured me, putting the instrument to her lips. "The Star-Spangled Banner" would ring out.

Conversations died down around us, and she performed even more passionately, finishing the patriotic number with her customary trills and embellishments.

There was often a pause while the restaurant patrons wondered how to react, and then the applause started up, and my mother beamed—she was always happiest in front of an audience, putting on a show.

But the threat of danger never faded, the feeling that we were one step away from disaster, with no one to catch us if we fell.

That summer, she announced, "Your mother is really going to have to pull off a miracle this time!"

"Why?" I asked, my stomach tightening.

She let out a deep sigh. "I didn't want to tell you about this, honey, because you know I don't like bad-mouthing your father in front of you, but I sent him a letter up in New York a few weeks ago, return receipt, which means he definitely got it. I told him how close we are to being homeless. And, of course, no reply. Can you believe that? No reply to the idea of his own daughter out on the street!"

I blinked. My first response was outrage—her outrage. It passed to me through osmosis, the way all her feelings did.

But really, it was no surprise. The Sperm Donor had struck again.

And it was no surprise that the person who wanted so badly to be the hero of my story was part of the reason I needed to be saved.

The next weekend, my friend from camp and I went to see *Batman*. I'd only heard about the caped crusader from pop culture references—he was a goofy, cartoon-ish, spandexed crime fighter, who made loud *POW!* and *BAM!* noises soar through the air. I had no idea of what really happened to Bruce Wayne.

I watched—awestruck—as Bruce became Batman, but I was horrified whenever either of them faced the Joker. Joker's compulsion to broadcast his pain so that it surrounded him as much as it grew inside him, to wreak havoc until not even a single citizen could breathe easy, not even for a moment; his obsession with deadly pranks and his insatiable need for the world to *look at him* . . . whenever he was onscreen, my body was ice. He was so scarred by anger and pain, so twisted in his definition of right and wrong, that he could justify frightening people within an inch of their lives just to make himself feel less alone.

The Joker was terrifying—and relentless—but it was Batman who truly moved me.

It was amazing to see this man use his fear of losing someone he loved to become more powerful, and not less. If Bruce Wayne could build something so strong upon so battered a foundation, could *anyone*?

It was unbelievable.

It was a lifeline.

Halfway through the film, when Batman first brings Vicki Vale into the Batcave, she notices all the real, live bats hanging from the ceiling, and says, softly, "Bats."

There's a pause, then Batman answers her, a world of words in just three: "They're great survivors."

I fell completely, head over heels, in love.

It was October 1991, and I was a sophomore in high school—all I could think about was the boy I'd spent freshman year obsessing over and the fact that he'd graduated the previous spring. It was a few days before this particular boy's birthday and I was on the phone with my best friend, Debi. My mother was late coming home from her boyfriend's apartment, but I wasn't concerned. It was much more important to prove to Debi that my romantic anguish was, in fact, unbearable.

At one point, I heard a strange noise outside my bed-

room window. I almost walked over to peek out the
blinds, but I was feeling too comfortable and too lazy.

A few hours later, the door to our apartment banged
open. It wasn't my mother—it was her boyfriend. He
grabbed the phone out of my hand and hung it up, then
told me to come with him.

I sat rigid in his car as we drove to an unknown desti-
nation, my questions unanswered. Eventually we arrived
at a police station. It was small and dirty, nothing like
the impressive police department I'd seen in Gotham
City. I looked around, taking in the hefty desk sergeant,
the officers taking up space, the peeling posters on the
walls. There were no warm, intelligent faces like Commissioner Gordon's looking out into the room. I shrank
into myself, scared and disgusted. My mother's boyfriend
walked over and said something to one of the officers,
who then led us into another room, narrow and filled with
a single long table.

There, sitting alone, was my mother. Her face was
blotchy, her clothing disheveled. When she saw me, her
face crumpled and fresh tears spilled down her cheeks.
She threw herself at me, folding my body into hers.
"I love you, I love you," she murmured into my hair.

I held her back, stunned and confused.

Finally, she pulled away and looked me in the eye. "We
can go home soon, honey," she said, her voice breaking.
"I just—I have to go to the hospital for a test."

We spent the rest of the night in the waiting area of
the emergency room, and the details were filled in for

me. My mother had been carjacked by two men—at gunpoint—when she'd pulled into her parking spot outside our apartment building that evening. They drove around for several hours, eventually stopping at a bank to withdraw the pitiful balance in her checking account. Then one man got in the backseat with her and sexually assaulted her, keeping the gun pressed into her back. They debated whether or not to kill her, but finally dumped her on a quiet road by the woods. She was able to flag down another car, then she called her boyfriend before 911, because the carjackers had her keys, and her only thought was making sure someone else got to me before they did.

The police never found the men responsible, and it wasn't until months later that I remembered the noise I'd ignored right outside my bedroom window. The window that looked out over the parking lot of our apartment complex, directly above the handicapped spot where my mother always parked.

A year later, the *Batman* animated series debuted on TV, and I rediscovered the Dark Knight on a smaller screen. But this wasn't just another silly, sunshiny cartoon. The gorgeous, shadowy landscape of Gotham sprawled out before me, and there was Batman, inflicting dark justice on every twisted, corrupt villain in the city—Batman saving people the cops weren't able to save.

I felt a familiar thrill at every musical flourish, every

swish of his cape across rooftops, every captured criminal. But in the double episode, "Two-Face, Parts 1 and 2," there was something I didn't recognize.

The climax of the first episode is a showdown between Harvey Dent—Gotham's district attorney and Bruce Wayne's good friend—and a criminal Harvey's trying to take down. Batman appears in the thick of the action, ready to save the day. I was ready to watch it happen.

Then fate intervened. Harvey gets caught in a terrible accident before Batman can rescue him. The explosion leaves half of Harvey's face and body completely deformed, resulting in a horrific, monstrous appearance and ultimately in Harvey's descent into madness, into the identity of the villain Two-Face.

For the first time since Bruce had become Batman, he'd failed to protect someone he loved. I was shocked and confused. In the second episode, Batman suffers through a nightmare in which Harvey asks over and over again, "Why couldn't you save me?" Harvey's apparition transforms into Bruce's parents, who repeat Harvey's question: "Why couldn't you save us, son?"

Watching Batman fail didn't weaken his influence over me—it made him loom larger. I no longer simply admired Batman. I felt he understood me in a way no one else did.

My mother held together the pieces of our world the best she could, shutting out the post-traumatic stress disorder of her assault, struggling to get me through high school and off to college in New York before facing the reality that she could no longer work a job with her crumbling spine. I was a sophomore in college when I got the phone call from Baltimore—she'd finally filed for disability and suffered a nervous breakdown.

"The doctors have decided on electroshock therapy," her friend told me over long distance. "They've tried different medications, but nothing's working. The depression is too strong. Your mother . . . she's barely even speaking."

I was overcome with fear, for my own future as much as for hers. I'd been lost in my head for months, fighting a depression that was all the more terrifying for its echoes of my mother's sickness. Hearing the doctors say that machines would be more effective than *people* at bringing my mother back was what tipped the scales—it shoved me off a ledge already constructed of crumbs.

I hung up and sat on my dorm room bed, unable to cry, unable to do anything but blink. Suddenly my roommate was there in front of me, telling me I had to get ready—a few of us were headed over to her brother's apartment for lunch.

I hadn't known it was possible to feel completely numb and completely afraid at the same time, but that's exactly how I felt on the subway ride to Julie's brother's apartment, and while sitting on his sofa, listening to everyone talk and laugh all around me.

I scanned the bookshelves that lined his living room

walls, taking in the huge collection of graphic novels. A
spark connected inside me.

"You know, I love Batman, but I've never read any Batman comics," I said to Julie's brother. "What would you recommend?"

He looked at me, paused, considered, then reached up and pulled out one of the slimmest volumes on the shelf. *Batman: The Killing Joke.*

I flinched at the cover image, a huge close-up of Joker with his wild green curls, his grin stretched wide, holding up a camera trained on us, the readers, and directing one chilling word of dialogue our way: "Smile."

I opened to the first page and read the story of how the Joker came to be—of the crushing loss that led him to his dark place. Spliced into these flashbacks was a tale set in the present, of the Joker committing the most brutal, devastating crime ever seen in a *Batman* comic.

Determined to prove that *any* man could become the Joker if pushed far enough, our villain visits Commissioner Gordon's home and makes Gordon watch as he shoots Gordon's daughter, Barbara, in the back, leaving her paralyzed.

I kept reading, standing at the foot of the bookshelves.

The Joker then kidnaps Gordon and brings him to a deserted fun house, torturing him with photos of Barbara lying naked and bleeding on the floor, teasing and prodding Gordon toward madness.

I waited, my entire body tense, as Batman tracked Joker to the fun house, and I felt the fear clamp down as

Batman arrived at the hall of mirrors, hearing Joker's triumphant proclamation: "I've demonstrated there's no difference between me and everyone else."

Batman hunts him down, and Joker continues to taunt him, chuckling through the words that nearly stopped my heart. "All it takes is one bad day to reduce the sanest man alive to lunacy."

Joker knew Bats had lived through an impossible, life-altering bad day—just as the Joker had—and the trauma had formed both of them into what and who they were.

"You had a bad day once, am I right?" The words appeared on the page next to an image of Batman, dangling over a floor of bloody spikes, gritting his teeth and holding on to a ledge with one hand. "You had a bad day and everything changed."

She did. I did.

It did.

Joker, Batman, Barbara, Commissioner Gordon, they were victims of inevitable circumstances, of horrible events powerful enough to break a person. Could anyone who lived that close to a tragedy—causing it, experiencing it, witnessing it, or being helpless to prevent it—come out the other side?

Batman pulls himself up onto the platform, takes off running, ignoring the Joker's heckling. In one single panel Batman bursts through a mirror, shards of glass flying everywhere, and grabs the Joker, fighting back, every word and every blow a rejection of the Joker's insanity. He tells him that he found Gordon, and despite everything the Joker had done to him, the commissioner was still in control. Heartbroken, but sane.

"Maybe ordinary people don't always crack," Batman says.

I shivered.

Consumed by grief, gutted by guilt, and always afraid that he could never make his iconic father proud, Batman turned his pain to power. His life was a mirror of the Joker's, but a mirrored reflection is also . . . an opposite. Batman proved that madness does not, *must* not, always breed more madness.

Sometimes, it breeds the antidote.

Batman's words filled my heart with hope, with a lightness and clarity. It wasn't a revelation but more of an affirmation.

I turned the page, wondering whether Batman would finally cross the line and kill the Joker. But rather than let his anger take over, Batman asks the Joker to let him help, to work together to find a path back to reason. Joker tells him it's too late, and shares a classic joke about two madmen: one tries to convince the other to cross between two buildings on the beam of his flashlight. But the second man refuses—what if the first man turns off the flashlight while he's halfway across?

The Joker breaks into his manic laughter, and at first, Batman just watches, stoic. Then a small laugh escapes, and then more, until the story ends with the two men collapsed together, laughing at a shared, horrific joke.

* * *

I returned to my dorm that night and called my mother's friend. "There's something they should know . . . before they try electroshock therapy." My voice was calm. "My mother has heart problems. Make sure you tell them."

Ultimately, the doctors held off on the treatment, and over time, she emerged from the catatonic state on her own. The physical and emotional pain she carried could never be erased, nor could its effects. But she found her way back to her jokes, to laughing more often than she cried.

And I came to understand why she needed those jokes. And how to laugh at them, too.

My friends only smile when I insist that Batman takes care of me, but then I'll receive an unexpected Batman-themed gift in the mail on a particularly bad day, or walk past someone wearing a shirt emblazoned with a giant bat symbol while heading to a doctor's appointment.

Is it really all that crazy to believe the Dark Knight is out there watching over me? Maybe I don't live in Gotham. Maybe he has bigger battles to fight. And maybe he can't be in two places at once. But the way I see it, Batman has always been the parent I needed, and the parent I had.

My favorite moment in any *Batman* comic is the opening of chapter three in *Batman: Year One*. First, it's the visual knockout punch that always gives me chills—bats swarming over and above the moon, increasing in number, coalescing into total blackness at the very top. Against this shot are the words: "They've got him CORNERED. They've got him OUTNUMBERED. They've got him TRAPPED. They're in TROUBLE . . ."

Looking at this image, a delicious comfort surrounds me, embraces me. For a moment, I experience the limitless faith and trust in a supreme being who is bigger than me, bigger than everyone and everything that could hurt me—whose mere existence in the world is enough to make me safe.

ACKNOWLEDGMENTS

First and foremost, thank you, Stephen Barr. To call you my agent seems like a gigantic understatement, because truly you are my coeditor. This entire anthology was your idea; and your legwork to bring contributors on board, your enthusiasm and care at every turn, and your wise edits were all invaluable.

Thank you to all of the essayists, particularly for your patience with me as I attempted to juggle this anthology alongside the first year of life with a newborn.

To Brendan Deneen, for sharing the vision for what this book could be and championing it at Thomas Dunne Books/St. Martin's Press, and Nicole Sohl, for all her help. To James Iacobelli, for a cover that exceeded my wildest hopes and to Laura Clark, Gabrielle Gantz, Christine Catarino, Sally Richardson, Thomas Dunne, and everyone at Thomas Dunne Books/St. Martin's Press, whose valuable work on this book is deeply appreciated.

To Reuben, for being this book's biggest cheerleader (second only to Stephen!) from the start. (And for being my oldest and best Super Friend.)

Dallas Mayr, this book wouldn't exist without you. I will never forget your advice: since Batman was a comfort to me, and writing was a comfort to me, then I should . . . write about Batman. Those pages and pages I wrote back then (which ultimately led to my essay in this collection) helped me make it through one of the hardest times in my life.

Bob Kane, Bill Finger, Alan Moore, Brian Bolland, Frank Miller, David Mazzuchelli, Paul Dini, Bruce Timm, Michael Uslan, and so many others . . . thank you for Batman.

James "Jack Abrams" Mignogna—love of my life, partner in crime, my very best friend. The greatest gift *Batman* ever brought me was you.